FRESHWATER

The Upper Thames
BILL TAYLOR

ERNEST BENN LIMITED · LONDON

First published as 'The Upper Thames' 1960

Second impression 1963

Second edition first published 1968
by Ernest Benn Limited
Bouverie House · Fleet Street · London · EC4

© L. W. TAYLOR 1968

Printed in Great Britain
510-25401-2

FRESHWATER FISHING
The Upper Thames

Also in this series

FRESHWATER FISHING: BIRMINGHAM AND WEST MIDLANDS

FRESHWATER FISHING: THE LOWER THAMES

THE LOCHS OF SCOTLAND

FISHING IN WALES

FISHING IN THE ISLE OF MAN

FISHING FOR LONDONERS

FISHING FOR SHEFFIELDERS

FISHING THE NORFOLK BROADS

ENGLISH RESERVOIRS

Contents

1. Where to Fish — 7
2. Float-fishing Methods — 26
3. Legering and Bite Detection — 34
4. Match Fishing the Thames — 48
5. Choosing a Swim — 56

Maps

Lechlade to Eynsham — 10

Wolvercot to Appleford — 16

Burcot to Mapledurham — 20

Reading to Marlow — 22

Marlow to Egham — 24

Illustrations

(*Between pages 32 and 33*)
A nice pike
148½lb of bream
Netting a bream
Match in progress
Famous roach swim at Donnington Bridge
Legering
A Thames barbel
A mixed bag
A near 7lb. bream

IN TEXT

Twin bodied float	30
Shotting the line	30
Link leger	37
Simple loop leger	37
Paternoster	37
The swim-feeder	37
The Ariel float	43
A simple bite indicator	43
Swing tip bite indicator	43
Setting up free float tackle	46
Fishing the free float	46

ACKNOWLEDGEMENT
Photographs by courtesy of *Angling Times*.

1. Where to Fish

THE UPPER Thames is without doubt one of the most beautiful and interesting stretches of river in the world. The lower Thames too, of course, wears an air of romance, the romance of politics in Westminster, money in the city, and the tales of old watermen at Wapping. Great ships and seabirds, mud flats and haunts of latter day smugglers all add to its allure.

But we can leave this without regret, for ours is the Thames that flows quietly between rushy banks, through water meadows, past wooded slopes and, boiling, over the sills of green weeded weirs. Our stretch too is steeped in history—and what is perhaps more important to you and me, it is full of fish. The historical names of Cricklade, Lechlade, Kelmscott, Shifford, Oxford, Dorchester, Goring and Henley bring to mind not so much ancient battles but, present day roach swims, fat chub and bream, sturdy barbel—and, I am afraid, swans! To the visitor intent upon enjoying the delights of the Thames Valley, the swans undoubtedly add beauty and interest. They, too, have their records in antiquity, for the seven thousand or so swans which now inhabit the river are descendants of wild birds native to the creek and estuary lands which became domesticated around about the reign of Richard I. If Richard I was really responsible he will not be blessed by anglers, for there is now scarcely a stretch of the river where one can be free from their unwelcome attentions.

It is inevitable that such an attractive stretch of water will appeal to people other than anglers, particularly during the summer months. It abounds in picturesque settings, ideal for bathing and picnic parties, and the amount of boat traffic seems to increase each year in spite of the fact that boat licence and lock dues on each of its forty-four locks (whether the boats go over, through or around!) make it one of England's most expensive pleasure rivers.

However, with the coming of September most of the river

traffic disappears and the angler enjoys comparative solitude and the best part of the fishing year. One can fish for a whole day without seeing another soul, the roach come plump and silver to the net, the bream perhaps feed madly for a while and the odd chub or barbel is an ever present possibility. At such times life is indeed good.

In winter, however, the Thames has certain drawbacks, not least of which is its unfortunate tendency to flood the banks during any spell of prolonged wet weather. A great deal of the Thames Valley disappears under a sheet of water and the angler is often hard put to find a reasonable swim. It is interesting to note that the average daily flow over Teddington Weir of 17,000,000 gallons may be increased fourfold during winter.

In spite of its vicissitudes it remains a river to delight the eye and gladden the heart of any coarse fisherman. It can be heartbreaking, but its rewards can be sufficient to satisfy even the most discriminating angler. Let us then get down to fish and fishing.

The whole of the non-tidal section of the Thames, from Cricklade to Teddington, is controlled by the Thames Conservancy and fishing is subject to the Thames Fishing by-laws, 1914. Most of the fishing above Staines is privately owned and is generally leased to angling societies. A copy of the by-laws, under review 1968, can be obtained from the Thames Conservancy Offices, 2/3 Norfolk Street, London, W.C.2. For the sake of the visiting angler, I include a list of those sections most applicable:—

(1) Rods and lines can only be used with natural or artificial baits designed to hook the fish in the mouth.
(2) Each angler is limited to two rods, which must not be more than fifteen feet apart.
(3) Terminal tackle must not include more than three separate baits.
(4) Tackle must not be left unattended with hook or bait in the water.
(5) Landing nets must not be more than two feet in diameter and three feet deep.
(6) Night fishing from a boat is forbidden.
(7) Night fishing is not allowed above Staines.
(8) No tackle is allowed which does not enable fish caught to be returned to the water without serious injury.

WHERE TO FISH

If you want to use a boat on the Thames, make sure that it is licensed.

Thames size limits below which every fish must be returned to the water immediately are:—

Barbel	Extreme	length	16	inches
Bleak	,,	,,	4	,,
Bream	,,	,,	12	,,
Carp	,,	,,	12	,,
Chub	,,	,,	12	,,
Dace	,,	,,	7	,,
Gudgeon	,,	,,	5	,,
Perch	,,	,,	9	,,
Pike	,,	,,	18	,,
Roach	,,	,,	8	,,
Rudd	,,	,,	8	,,
Tench	,,	,,	10	,,
Trout	,,	,,	16	,,

Close Seasons:—
Coarse fish — 15 March to 15 June
Trout — 11 September to 31 March

Unlike most River Boards the Thames Conservancy do not issue licenses covering the river. Payment of the club fee or permission from the owners of the fishery is all that is required.

Permits to go upon weirs are issued by the Thames Conservancy but are subject to existing private fishing or other rights. At the majority of weirs, no objection is raised by the owners of fisheries to persons fishing.

Permits cost £1 per year and expire 31 December.

Here is a list of weirs from the upper Thames downstream:—

Grafton Weir	Sutton Weir	Bray Weir
Radcott Weir	Day's Weir	Boveney Weir
Rushey Weir	Cleeve (Upper Weir)	Romney Weir
Shifford Weir	Goring Weir	Old Windsor Weir
Eynsham Weir	Shiplake Weir	Bell Weir
Sandford Weir	Marsh Weir	Shepperton Weir
	Hambledon Weir	Sunbury Weir
	Marlow Weir	Molesey Weir

The first important stretch of the Thames is from Cricklade

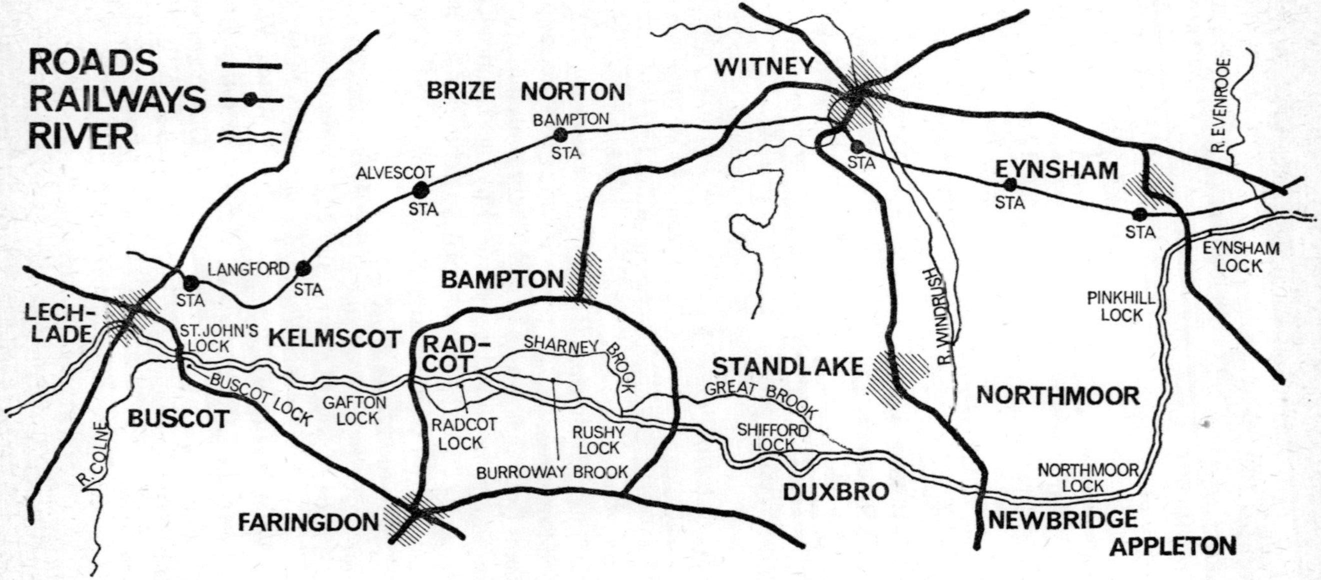
ROADS
RAILWAYS
RIVER
BRIZE NORTON
WITNEY
R. EVENROOE
BAMPTON
STA
ALVESCOT
STA
LANGFORD
STA
STA
EYNSHAM
STA
STA
STA
EYNSHAM LOCK
PINKHILL LOCK
BAMPTON
LECH-LADE
ST. JOHN'S LOCK
KELMSCOT
RAD-COT
SHARNEY BROOK
R. WINDRUSH
STANDLAKE
NORTHMOOR
GREAT BROOK
BUSCOT LOCK
GAFTON LOCK
BUSCOT
RADCOT LOCK
RUSHY LOCK
SHIFFORD LOCK
R. COLNE
BURROWAY BROOK
DUXBRO
NORTHMOOR LOCK
FARINGDON
NEWBRIDGE
APPLETON

to Lechlade. On this reach the infant Thames is joined by its tributaries the Ray, Church, Colne and Cole. This stretch offers some excellent roach fishing; chub are numerous and the occasional bag of bream is taken too.

The Trout Inn at Lechlade provides an excellent centre and owns the water upstream, to Round House, Inglesham, mouth of the River Colne and downstream to Lord Faringdons Boathouse about a mile below Buscot Weir. Both St. John's and Buscot Weir are included and do not come under the Thames Conservancy Weir permit. A permanent bailiff is in residence and day tickets are available from him (Trout 3/6d. Coarse fish 3/-).

Weekly and season tickets are also available. Accommodation is available at the Inn, excellent meals are available, also snacks at the bar.

On the trout water, which is, incidentally, all fishable from the banks, the angler has a wide choice of swims ranging from weirs to slow, deep water. It holds an excellent head of fish, including good barbel and bream. The chub fishing in the weir pools can be exceptionally good (fish to $5\frac{1}{2}$ lb.) and pike are numerous. For the enthusiast keen to catch a Thames trout this water offers excellent opportunity.

Fishing the side of the island opposite the Inn I have had some excellent bags of chub long-trotting under the bank.

Both banks of the three mile stretch from Lord Faringdon's Boathouse downstream to the lower end of Grafton Weir are owned by the landlord of 'The Anchor Inn' at Eaton Hastings. This inn caters particularly for anglers and is justifiably popular. Day tickets at 3/6d. and season tickets at 30/- are available from the landlord, Mr. D. A. Liggins, who welcomes parties of anglers and arranges club contests and competitions. Boat moorings and a camping site are available, and riverside caravans may be rented.

Downstream from Grafton Weir Pool we come to Radcot Bridge, another good fishing centre. The water between the two locks, approximately two and a quarter miles (both banks), is owned by the Radcot Angling Club. Day tickets at 2/6d. are available from the Proprietor of the Swan Hotel—Mr. J. Bowl. A bream of 9 lb. was taken from this water in 1959.

Below Radcot is the delightfully named Tadpole Bridge and the Trout Inn there issues day tickets for the stretch from

Rushey Weir (not including the Weir apron) down to the Tenfoot Bridge, a distance of three miles, one mile upstream, two miles downstream. Vic Stevens, the landlord, is an angler who knows his water and, regrettably rare in these days, one who goes out of his way to make the visiting angler welcome. As he says 'A large percentage of our trade comes from the angler and I have always tried to maintain the atmosphere of an Anglers' Pub . . .' although some extensive alterations are taking place muddy gumboots will always be welcome.

There is an extensive camping site alongside the river; 2/6d. per tent per night, and a very large car-park. The Inn does quite a lot of snack-type catering—hot pies, eggs, bacon, chips etc., and full course meals for parties. A cup cup of tea can be available on arrival (if not *too* early!), and on departure.

Bream do not predominate on this water and if they are taken in any quantity or size, it is usually under adverse conditions with the river virtually in flood. The banks are very high and the river can accommodate six feet or more of floodwater. It is thought that in these conditions bream come upstream for some protection.

The barbel have really established themselves and, as well as containing a quite prolific head of fish up to between 3 and 5 lb. of fish over 10 lb. have been taken. There are many tales of anglers being well and truly 'smashed up'. I visited this stretch during the 1967 Thames Championship and saw one fine fish of about 8 lbs. in the net whilst a little further downstream an angler played and lost one estimated to be in the region of 10 lb.

There are, of course, plenty of chub, but the really big boys (as elsewhere!) are very wary indeed. In common with many parts of the upper Thames, this reach seems to be losing its shoals of sizeable roach, but good bags are still taken, dace reckon to be on the increase and as Vic Stevens says 'when the gudgeon first take they have you reaching for the landing net!'

Adjoining this water, above Rushey Weir, and opposite Radcot waters, is a stretch leased by Coventry and District Angling Association. They do not issue day tickets but their Association Book is on general sale at £1. This is an excellent mixed fishery. The last time I fished it with Billy Lane in search of the bream, I had barbel, and Bill had, of all things, tench!

It will be noticed from the map that below Tadpole a backwater forms a loop on the southern side of the Thames, headed by Shifford Weir. This portion of the old Thames is a most beautiful stream, reminiscent of the Windrush. Though it looks primarily a roach and chub water, I have seen bream of 6 lbs. and over taken from one of its deeper stretches.

Newbridge is a very popular venue for visiting anglers and day tickets are available from both its famous Inns, the Maybush and the quaintly named 'Rose Revived'. The Maybush water offers a variety of fishing. The last time I fished it I was really concerned with doing some punting and fishing scenes for a film on the Thames which was being made by a German film company. On these occasions one must usually give up any idea of serious angling and fit in the required scenic pattern. On this occasion we were having trouble with the light as the sun refused to shine for more than a few moments at a time. Fed up with hanging around, I pushed the punt into a little bay just above the Inn, flicked a few maggots into the stream, and started trotting down. Within an hour I had ten pounds or so in my net, consisting of chub to 3 lb., sizeable roach and plump little dace.

Across the bridge at the 'Rose Revived Inn' day tickets are available for the Thames (3/6d.) and for the Windrush (5/-) which joins the Thames at this point. No charge for fishing is made to hotel guests.

Visitors to the Thames are likely to be attracted to some of its tributaries, and perhaps I should mention here that other ticket water on the Windrush is available to residents of the well-known Bull Hotel at Burford, seven day tickets (10/-) are available from Burford Angling Society to visitors to Burford and locality during the period,

This beatifully named stream is one of the prettiest I have ever fished and, in addition to its scenic charm, it offers fishing of a very high quality indeed. Chub and dace are the main quarry, but the roach, when you find them, are of a pleasing size. The dace, I risk saying, are as good as any you will find anywhere. The general size is large and fish of a pound are by no means unusual, in fact, I fished in a match once where the winner included two dace over the pound in his bag. The chub are chunky fish too and as usual, great care is required if you are to contact the big chaps.

There are trout present, but from my own experience I

should think it fair to say that they are few and far between. Because of the nature of the water they are usually fished for with minnow—the latter being plentiful—rather too plentiful for the maggot angler.

Since I have not mentioned minnow fishing elsewhere, I should say that this method is deadly for chub as well as trout, and I have also used it widely on the Thames when minnows have been readily available. My method is to use a 3 to 5 lb. line, a No. 6 to 10 hook tied directly to the line, and a scrap of rough cork for a float. I usually bore a small hole in the latter and, after passing the line through it, I jam it with a matchstick or piece of twig. Lead shot may be used on the trace, but I avoid it, usually finding that the minnow will swim down into deeper water providing the trace is long enough. I usually fish the minnow alive (lip-hooked) though it works quite well with dead bait, and I know that Peter Stone has taken a lot of barbel on this method. Bites, when they come (whether from chub, trout or barbel) are positively vicious and, unless you are quick on the strike, you will regularly find yourself reeling in nothing but the head of the minnow!

Before leaving Newbridge, it is of interest to mention that during the close season one may often see shoals of spawning barbel in the Windrush, just above the bridge.

The river from Newbridge to Northmoor Lock is renowned for its roach fishing but also holds the usual run of Thames fish including, of recent years, large bream. The water from above the lock to one gate below is owned by Oxford Angling and Preservation Society who issue day and visitors tickets for some of their water. I have always thought that this stretch offers some of the best roach fishing on the upper Thames and have spent some very happy days there in pursuit of that species. I remember on one rather quiet day when fishing there with Bert Lewis of Oxford, I visited his swim to see how he was making out. I do not think I have ever seen such a disconsolate angler. He sat there examining his broken line and, unfortunately, I missed the action which led to the 'smash-up' by a fraction of a minute. Finding the roach hard to please he was fishing very lightly with an 18 hook and single maggot in a very deep run. His float dipped, and on striking he felt what he took to be a gudgeon. As he reeled it in it was snatched by a very large fish which he then played for some time. Suddenly the water parted and a huge trout (possibly 10 lb.) showed itself momentarily before disappearing with his terminal tackle, float and all. Anything can happen on the Thames!

The water below Northmoor Lock to Bablock Hythe Ferry is owned by Appleton & Tubney A.S. who do not issue day tickets. This is again primarily a roach water with the occasional shoal of bream.

From Bablock Hythe downstream the towpath crosses to the opposite side of the river and for several miles downstream the fishing rights are owned by Oxford Angling and Preservation Society.

On the opposite side there is a stretch owned by The Chequers Inn, Bablock Hythe, and day tickets are available for one and a half miles of water at a cost of 5/- per day. This water holds an excellent head of coarse fish and is renowned for the splendid bags of barbel which are taken each season. Bream, too, are present, and the shoals are large, with fish of a good average size. This is another of my favourite roach fisheries and I think that my best ever catch of quality Thames roach was taken here late one evening.

On the towpath side the Oxford Angling and Preservation Societies' water extends down past Pink Hill Weir and Eynsham Bridge to a point above King's Weir, known as Carrot's Ham. This stretch of water has become renowned in recent years as the home of really big bream, fish of 6 lb. being by no means uncommon. Matches are quite often won with bags of around 100 lb. and individual pleasure anglers (of which I have been one!) have taken huge hauls. Interestingly enough it was from a swim between Eynsham Bridge and Carrot's Ham that J. J. Perkins took the record brace of bream in 1928. These fish weighed 10 lb. $13\frac{1}{2}$ oz. and 9 lb. $14\frac{1}{2}$ oz. respectively. I have seen these fish in their case (the size of a small piano!) and they really are a sight to stir the blood of a bream angler.

As well as bream, this water holds a good selection of fish of other species and, on days when the bream are off, it is quite likely that a match will be won with two or three good barbel. Before the bream became quite as prolific as they are Carrot's Ham was another renowned area for roach fishing.

The reach from Carrot's Ham down to the Trout Inn at Godstow is controlled by North Oxford Angling Association and as their terms of renting prohibit sub-letting, no day tickets

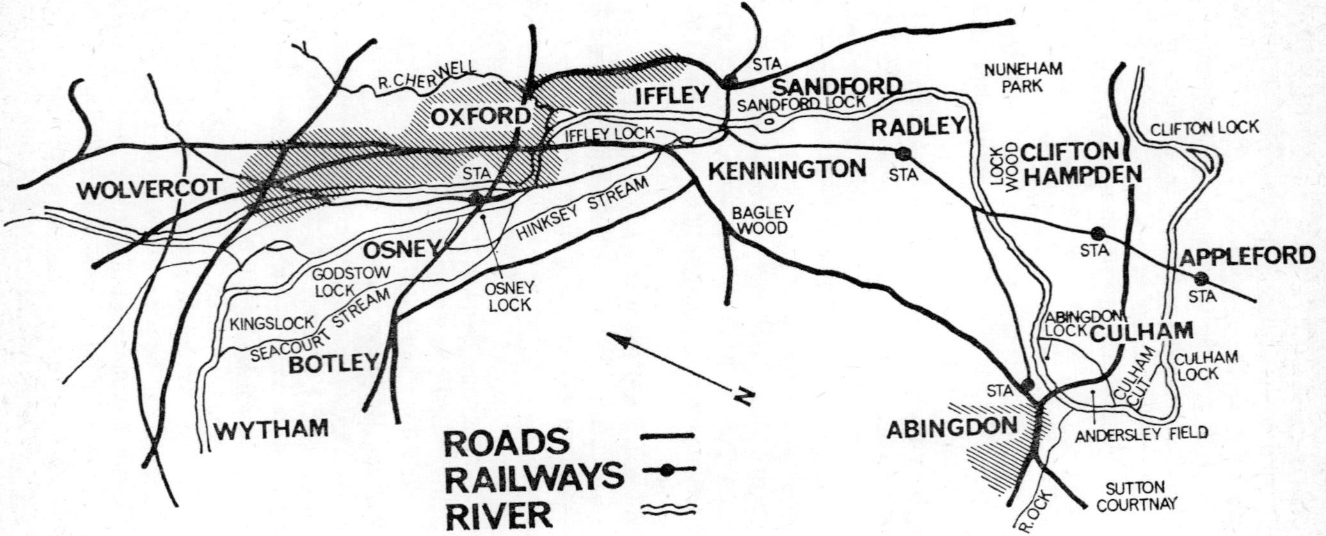
R. CHERWELL
OXFORD
IFFLEY
STA
SANDFORD
SANDFORD LOCK
NUNEHAM
PARK
RADLEY
CLIFTON LOCK
LOCK
WOOD
CLIFTON
HAMPDEN
WOLVERCOT
STA
IFFLEY LOCK
KENNINGTON
STA
HINKSEY STREAM
BAGLEY
WOOD
OSNEY
GODSTOW
LOCK
OSNEY
LOCK
STA
APPLEFORD
STA
KINGSLOCK
SEACOURT STREAM
BOTLEY
N
ABINGDON
LOCK
CULHAM
CULHAM
CUT
CULHAM
LOCK
STA
ABINGDON
ANDERSLEY FIELD
WYTHAM
ROADS
RAILWAYS
RIVER
R. OCK
SUTTON
COURTNAY

are available. This reach includes the well known Kings Weir, one of the nicest weirs to fish I know of on the whole of the Thames. It holds very good chub and barbel, and seems to offer a great attraction to bream, too, in the early part of the season. One used to be able to fish Kings on a weir permit but I notice that its name has been dropped from my most up-to-date list.

The water, from Godstow for several miles down through Oxford, is free water, but much of it is controlled by Oxford and District Angling Association. Much of it is available to visiting individual anglers but coach parties must obtain prior permission. Day tickets are available on some waters; guest tickets are available from Oxford Angling & Preservation Society to members only, all other applications should be made to the secretary in writing. Tackle Dealers and sources of information on local fishing are:—

Fred Taylor, James Street, Oxford.
Arthur Smith, Magdalene Road, Oxford.
Venables & Co. St. Aldates, Oxford.

The water I am now describing is, to me, my home water, so the reader might forgive me if I add that I consider it to offer the best fishing on the whole of the Thames.

Situated at the top end of this water is the Trout Inn at Godstow, a very popular meeting place for Oxford Town & Gown and much favoured by visitors. I would not describe it as a fisherman's pub, but it is certainly worth a visit. It is situated on a small weir pool and a favourite occupation on summer evenings is to sit on the wall above the water casting down titbits for the huge shoal of chub which inhabit the pool. It really is a large shoal, and some of its members must be approaching the 6 lb. mark. Whopping old loggerheads, grown large upon a diet of sandwiches, pork pies, potato crisps and the odd cigarette end!

I had permission to fish the pool on a few occasions in my undergraduate days and, although I had some good fish, they were not nearly as easy to catch as one would expect from their nonchalant acceptance of free offerings. In fact, I found that the best bait was a live bleak fished on float tackle and, even then, after taking a couple of fish (smaller ones of course!) the shoal had to be 'rested' before any more could be taken.

The reach from Godstow down to the Bailey Bridge is known as The Medley, it is bordered by the towpath on one side and the famous Port Meadow on the other. This is a superb water, much of it is very wide and rather shallow in fact, though many references are made to its various 'bream holes' there is not one real hole in the length of it. In fact, apart from the odd bends and bays it could be said to be a somewhat featureless water. When I first fished it, years ago, most of its banks were sedge lined and rather attractive, but in succeeding years a good deal of the margin reed and weeds have been destroyed. I should say as a consequence of the ever increasing boat traffic.

When I lived in Oxford I spent countless hours on the Medley and, though I fished principally for bream in the summer and bream or roach in the winter, I have caught just about everything there, including a Thames Trout (albeit a small one) and, of all things, a grayling.

As a bream water it is outstanding—when you find them that is—for like all of this sometimes infuriating river, it is inclined to be patchy. I used to put in a great deal of time looking for the fish, up before dawn, walking or cycling along the towpath even before the season commenced, but it paid dividends; often large ones.

Occasionally during the winter, the bream may be located quite close to whichever bank you may be fishing. With a bit of stream running the water takes on more character and becomes easier to read; obvious bream swims expose themselves and to this extent the fish are easier to locate (whether they will be prepared to feed is *quite* a different matter). In summer, however, the fish may be anywhere for although there are one or two of what I call 'holding swims' (areas where fish tend to congregate fairly regularly) they do spend a great deal of the time 'wandering'.

Whichever section of the river they happen to be in, it is most likely that they will be well out in the middle; long casting with leger tackle is the usual way to catch them.

One of the great mysteries of the Medley water is that of its barbel. Barbel are caught quite regularly and, in fact, the biggest barbel I have ever contacted (and that includes one of over 12 lb. from the Hampshire Avon) was on this very water. On that occasion I was match fishing for roach and took the barbel on double maggot, No. 16 hook and $2\frac{1}{4}$ lb. line. I lost the barbel after about twenty minutes and won the match with 20 lb. of prime roach. However, the mystery is that though the barbel can be seen in huge shoals during the close season, nobody ever seems to contact them in any quantity afterwards. I have taken many people to see the barbel spawning on the shallows just below the Trout Inn and believe me, it is a sight which shatters even non-anglers, row upon row, column upon column of splendid fish varying in size from perhaps 3 lb. to 10 lb. interspersed with the odd chub here and there. An acquaintance told me that, counting as accurately as he could, he viewed over 800 there one day and that number did not take into account those which were invisible in the deeper water.

My own theory is that once spawning is over they break into very small groups and spread themselves out. It is interesting to note that in the case of Thames barbel they are by no means restricted to the fast water and, in fact, many of them are taken from typical bream swims.

Half-way between the Trout and the Bailey Bridge is the hamlet of Binsey which offers a point of access to the water and a well-placed and aptly named pub, The Perch.

Just above the Bailey Bridge the river divides into two streams and the bridge marks the site of what was once a weir. The pool below the weir fishes extraordinarily well during the winter, and, in floodwater, I have taken bags of bream, roach, tench and even eels.

The backwater meanders off to eventually flow parallel to the Oxford canal; there are many such backwaters of the Thames in and around Oxford, many of which offer excellent fishing, some of it free. One of them, Pott's Stream, has become very well known for its huge barbel.

The mainstream down from the bridge to Botley Road is known as Medley Manor, the river is deeper and a good deal narrower than Medley and used to be particularly well known for its roach. It is from this water that I took what I believe is still a Thames record for four hour's individual fishing—148½ lb. of bream—forty-two fish including one of 7¼ lb. I have also had some very nice barbel along this stretch.

From Botley Road the river takes on a rather sordid appearance as it winds its way along by the Gasworks before emerging as the Isis; the famous boating stretch which extends to Iffley Lock. If you do not insist upon sylvan surroundings when fishing, then the Gasworks area offers some of the best roach fishing in

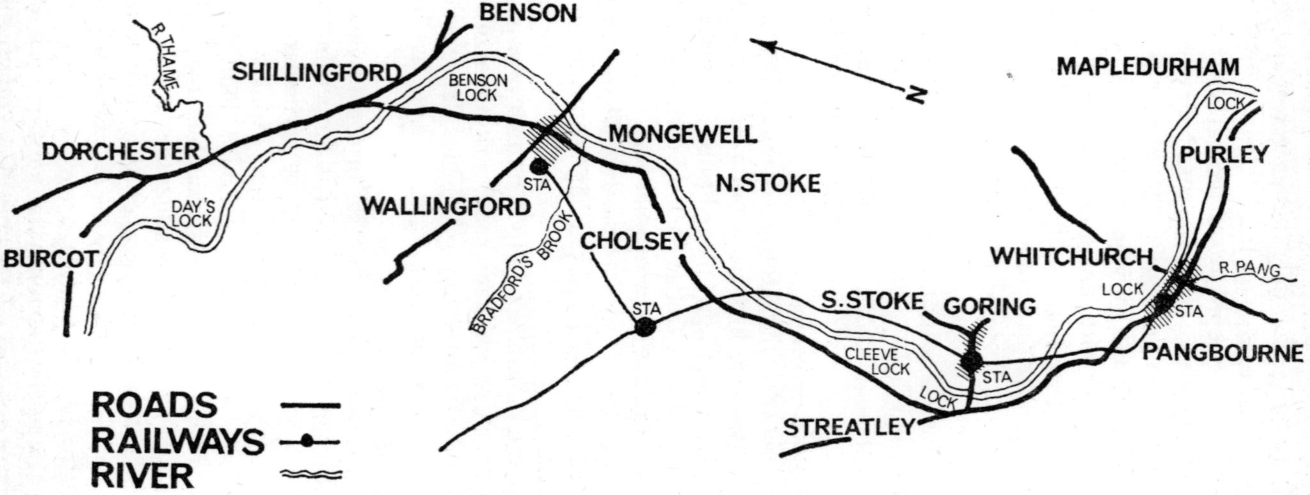
BENSON
R. THAME
SHILLINGFORD
BENSON LOCK
DORCHESTER
MONGEWELL
N. STOKE
MAPLEDURHAM
LOCK
PURLEY
N
DAY'S LOCK
STA
WALLINGFORD
BURCOT
CHOLSEY
BRADFORD'S BROOK
WHITCHURCH
R. PANG
LOCK
STA
S. STOKE
GORING
STA
PANGBOURNE
CLEEVE LOCK
STA
LOCK
STREATLEY
ROADS
RAILWAYS
RIVER

the area. I used to fish it quite a lot in winter and had some cracking bags of roach.

The Isis stretch offers good mixed fishing though roach predominate. In summer and during term time in winter too, boat traffic is a great nuisance.

The next main point of access below Iffley is Sandford and there is some fine fishing available there. The weir pool is a very large one and holds a very good mixed head of fish. I have had great sport there in summer fishing with weed from the sill of the weir. It is particularly well known for its barbel but, in addition, one hears most years of the capture of Thames trout.

From Sandford down to Clifton Hampden most of the water is in club hands though there is some free water available. The Oxford and District Angling Association owns a stretch of water downstream from the bridge but it is not particularly popular as it swarms with small bream. I have fished it many times without ever taking a bream over 1½ lb. though I have often had bags of 100 fish or more.

The Clifton and District Piscatorial Society have their headquarters at the lovely 'Barley Mow' and residents at the Inn or in the village on holiday may purchase a weekly visitors' ticket for 12/6d.

The Dorchester-Shillingford stretch has always been noted for its big bream and this reach offers some very exciting fishing. Warborough and Shillingford Angling Club allow day ticket fishing on their club water at 5/- per day. The secretary is Mr. P. G. Andrews, 6 Henfield View, Warborough, Oxford. The nearest pub to the water is The New Inn, Shillingford—an excellent hostelry!

Day tickets for water owned by the Jolly Angler, Wallingford, are 2/- each and are available from the local tackle dealer at the Town Arms Hotel. Waters are available on the Benson Reach, Oxford Reach, Chatmore Reach and the B.M.H. Reach. Coach parties are only allowed on application to the secretary four weeks in advance. Hempseed is strictly prohibited.

The river between Goring and Moulsford is very attractive and offers an interesting variety of fishing. Ye Olde Leather Bottel, a well-known riverside pub, owns two miles of fishing. Day tickets are 2/- and inclusive terms may be arranged for fishing residents.

At Reading, most of the water below the Whitchurch Bridge

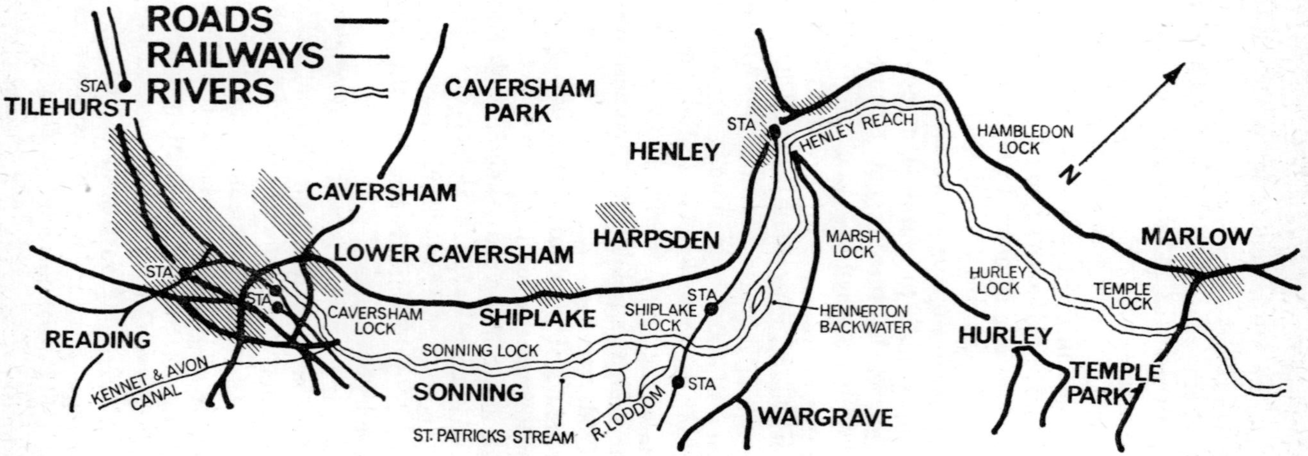

ROADS
RAILWAYS
RIVERS
STA
TILEHURST
CAVERSHAM PARK
CAVERSHAM
LOWER CAVERSHAM
READING
KENNET & AVON CANAL
STA
STA
CAVERSHAM LOCK
SONNING LOCK
SHIPLAKE
SONNING
ST. PATRICKS STREAM
HARPSDEN
HENLEY
STA
HENLEY REACH
SHIPLAKE LOCK
STA
R. LODDOM
STA
WARGRAVE
HENNERTON BACKWATER
MARSH LOCK
HAMBLEDON LOCK
N
HURLEY LOCK
HURLEY
TEMPLE LOCK
TEMPLE PARK
MARLOW

down to Tilehurst is either in the hands of clubs or permission has to be obtained from the owners. Below Tilehurst most of the fishing is owned by Reading Corporation. Individual anglers are allowed to fish there, but clubs wishing to fish matches there must obtain permission from the Corporation. The water at Caversham has the reputation for 'small-stuff'. Perhaps this reputation is undeserved, but on the only occasion I fished Caversham Reach (during one of the Thames Championships) I took ninety-seven roach, perch, and dace, without one sizeable fish to weigh!

From the Kennet's mouth to Sonning the owners do not exercise their rights and fishing is free. On the Kennet all fishing from the towpaths, from a point just above the Co-op Jam Factory at Reading to the first lock above Station Road at Theale, is under the control of the Reading and District Angling Association and in some places both banks are controlled.

Fishing rights are also held at East Towney, Padworth, Woolhampton and Midgeham. All fishing upstream from the first weir below Burghfield Bridge is available to members only, but from the weir back to the Jam Factory the public are allowed to fish free of charge from Monday to Friday inclusive: 3/- per day on Saturdays and Sundays.

Permission to fish from the opposite bank to the towing path may be obtained from the lock-keeper at Burghfield Bridge at a charge of 3/- per day. This water extends from Burghfield Bridge to Southcote Lock. Clubs wishing to fish matches on this water must obtain prior permission from the lock-keeper.

The tackle dealer in Reading is F. X. Eggleton, proprietor, Perry & Cox, 19 Kings Road, Reading.

My own feeling is that, on the whole, the fishing is better above Reading than below, but the length from Reading to Windsor does produce some excellent bags of fish.

The reach from Henley to Windsor can fairly claim to be the most beautiful on the Thames. At Henley, Marlow and Bourne End, fishing is free from all parts of the towpath. Though boats are a menace during the summer months these are popular resorts and good bags are taken. Again, the appearance of the ubiquitous bream has in some ways changed the nature of what were once thought of primarily as roach waters.

I am particularly fond of the river just above Henley; indeed I sometimes think that it epitomises Thames angling, excellent

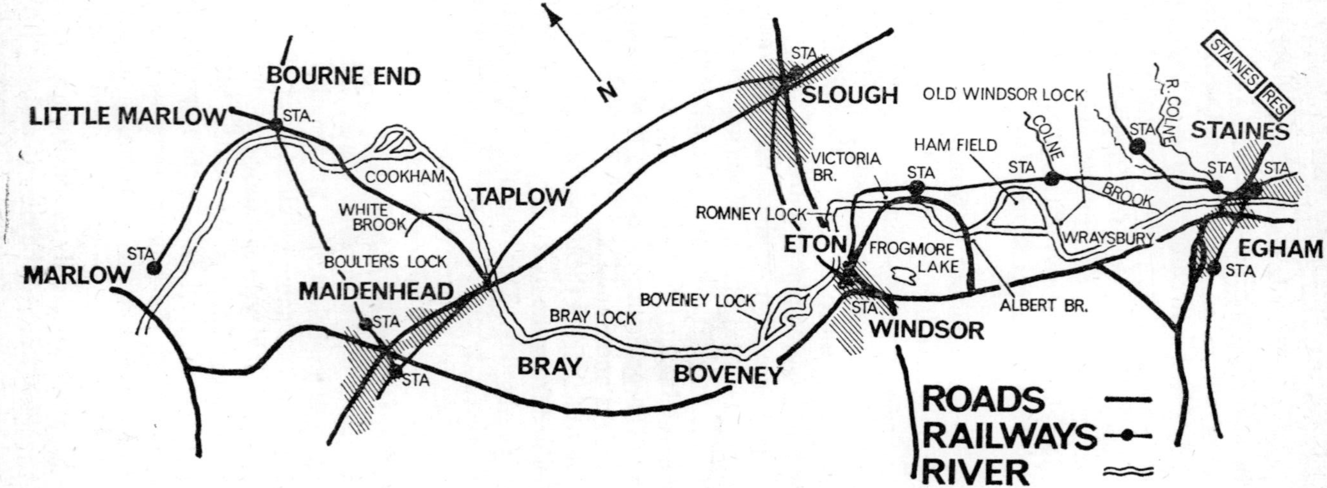

BOURNE END
LITTLE MARLOW
STA.
MARLOW
STA
COOKHAM
WHITE BROOK
BOULTERS LOCK
MAIDENHEAD
STA
STA
TAPLOW
N
BRAY
BRAY LOCK
BOVENEY LOCK
BOVENEY
SLOUGH
STA
VICTORIA BR.
ROMNEY LOCK
ETON
FROGMORE LAKE
STA
WINDSOR
OLD WINDSOR LOCK
HAM FIELD
STA
COLNE
STA
BROOK
WRAYSBURY
ALBERT BR.
STAINES RES
R. COLNE
STA
STAINES
STA
STA
EGHAM
STA
ROADS
RAILWAYS
RIVER

fishing in beautiful surroundings. Last time I fished there was on one of those autumnal days which seemed specially chosen for a fishing trip. I had the good fortune to contact a shoal of bream, whilst above me, two anglers, fishing from a punt, were catching roach after roach. A perfect day.

At Maidenhead much of the water is controlled by Maidenhead and District Angling Society whose clubroom is at the Rose Hotel, King Street, Maidenhead.

Local 'free' waters extend downstream from Brunels Bridge (The Sounding Arches) to Bray, by way of Bray Towpath, and upstream from Maidenhead Bridge to Cookham by way of Bridge Gardens; the road from the Boathouses up to Boulters Lock, and the Cookham Towpath from Boulters Lock up to My Lady Ferry.

The usual species are present, roach and dace being most common especially from the famous 'Wall' below the Sounding Arches. Perch and barbel are also caught, notably from 'the railings'. Bream are rare except down towards the Bray area.

Fishing is free from both banks at Windsor, except at private moorings. To the visiting angler who fancies a change from the Thames, there are some useful gravel pits in the area available on day tickets. Information is available from tackle dealers: R. Harding, 6 St. Leonards Road, Windsor.

2. Float-fishing Methods

TO ME there is no more delightful way of taking fish than on float fishing tackle. The sight of a well-balanced float gliding slowly down with the stream, or resting gently on the surface of some quiet backwater, is always a vision of promise. Once, when asked what I thought was the most exciting thing about angling, I decided that for me it was that moment which comes when I see the float dip and slide away; I strike, the float comes partly out of the water, and then the muscular lunge of a good fish is felt as the float slides beneath the surface again and the rod arches into action.

In the summer, unless it happens to be particularly cursed with heavy rainfall, the Thames is a very slow-moving river, and trotting the stream (if indeed there is any real stream to trot!) is a very leisurely process. Later in the year, when the stream speeds up a little, the man who wants to 'trot down' will be kept pretty busy. But this is the time when the float comes into its own and I am not deterred by the fact that it is a technique requiring the expenditure of some energy. It can be a very tiring process but undue fatigue can be avoided by choosing a well balanced outfit.

Although it is nice to have the right tackle for the job, I feel that sometimes too much attention is paid to highly specialised tackle with the result that anglers start off by feeling that they are handicapped because they do not possess some item of tackle exactly as specified by a modern day Isaac Walton. Let me give you some idea of tackle I have tried and then form your own conclusions.

I began by using a twelve foot match special. This had a top joint (four feet) of built cane and about eighteen inches of built cane spliced into the middle joint, the remainder of the rod being of Spanish Reed. It was in many ways a pleasant rod to use, being very light but still fairly powerful; I remember it with great affection. I would not *choose* such a rod today, Spanish

Reed has outlived its utility. Nevertheless, it amuses me to recall that at the time it was in service such rods were frequently described as 'useless' by the angling pundits, yet I had many good bags of roach, bream, and tench on it, and on one occasion (quite accidentally) a 7½ lb. pike. I eventually smashed the butt trying to pelt a light float halfway across the river in the teeth of a gale—those old match rods were not meant to stand up to prolonged bouts of 'whip' or 'punch' casting.

I next tried built cane rods—both hollow built and solid cane. Two of these I have found of special value and they are still the favourite weapons in my armoury after many years of sterling service. One is a 'Peter Tombleson Float Rod' made by James of Ealing. This is a twelve feet three inch, two joints with a separate butt. It was a very easy action right down to the butt—in fact one can throw a fly with it—and yet it is surprisingly powerful. I have had hundredweights of fish on this rod and yet it is still as good as the day *Angling Times* presented it to me for catching a load of bream. Because of its action I particularly like to use this rod with light tackle. In fact, fishing with this rod in the Hampshire Avon Championship one year, I hooked (on 2¼ lb. line and 16 hook) a salmon of about 12 lb. and beat it. It did take quite a long time!

The other rod was made for me by Chapmans of Ware to my own specification. This rod is thirteen feet long and much more powerful than the Tombleson, I use it mainly for bream, barbel or tench. It is rather a heavy rod for continuous trotting but it has a long narrow butt which tucks comfortably under the elbow thus taking most of the weight off the wrist.

Another rod which I have found very useful is the Apollo Taperflash. I think mine was amongst the first they made and, of course, since then they have become very popular. I know that some people are put off by the idea of using steel in a fishing rod (very often after trying ex army tank aerials which were widely advertised) but there is no doubt that modern methods produce a very fine piece of fishing tackle. Mine is a fourteen-footer which converts into a twelve footer too.

For the wider reaches, or when fishing deep water, I prefer a rod of fourteen feet and find I can handle it quite comfortably. The extra length is quite handy in picking up line when striking at a distance, and the action combines a swift strike with plenty of guts. The twelve footer feels like a wand in one's hands and is one of my favourite tools for roach fishing in waters of medium depth and width. I also find it to be an absolutely first-class leger rod.

Lastly, mention must be made of fibre-glass rods. There is a tremendous range of rods in this material available today and many of them are excellent. I think I used one of the very first prototypes of a hollow fibre-glass bottom rod to be seen in this country. That rod was rather 'sloppy' for my taste but, even so, I could forecast the trend that was to follow. Sportex, Milbro and Dunlop are three names which readily come to mind and, of course, there are many more. Though somewhat reluctantly, I cannot help thinking that any rod I buy in the future is more than likely to be manufactured from fibre-glass.

The next important question is that of line strength. On the whole, Thames anglers tend to fish 'heavy'—certainly by Midland and Northern standards. Of course there is a reason for it, Thames fish tend to be on the heavy side too!

One could write a whole chapter on the controversy surrounding line strengths and anyone who regularly reads the angling press will be aware of the many bitter battles waged over this issue. I shall contend myself with two points. One, the use of a light line can lead to a more delicate presentation of the bait, and this has little to do with the hoary old myth of the fish seeing, or not seeing, the line. Two, I fish as light as the conditions will allow because that is how I enjoy fishing, and fishing to me seems to be concerned with enjoyment. I use a $2\frac{1}{2}$ lb. line whenever I can, but go up to 5 lb. when seeking the large and powerful species, and up to 9 lb. for pike and the larger carp.

Generally speaking, when I am fishing I have one particular species in mind and fish accordingly. I should hate to catch my first 2 lb. roach on bream tackle!

I have yet to meet the angler who can resist the temptation to collect floats and there will be few reasonably equipped fishermen who do not already possess in their collection floats suitable for Thames fishing. Most of my own floats I have made from balsa wood, quills of all kinds, corks, cane and elder pith. I have designed all manner of shapes to suit varying conditions of wind and stream, but even with my varied collection I sometimes feel that I have not *quite* the float I want. For most purposes quills, particularly porcupine quills, in one size or another are ideal. I make a lot of balsa floats in either a quill or slim torpedo shape: I reckon to turn out a dozen and a half in about an hour and they cost me something like three-halfpence each.

Lastly, on the question of rods, I would suggest that unless you are an absolute ace at long casting with a centre-pin, a fixed spool rod will be a necessity for much of your fishing. A couple of spare spools filled to capacity with lines of different breaking strain will prove most useful.

As a visitor to the Thames you may notice that many of the 'Old Guard' fish quite close to the bank, often 'laying-on' or 'street-pegging' as it is called. This can be an effective method, particularly if you find a good depth of water close to the bank and a swim well away from the madding crowd. There are many such swims on the upper Thames, often with a line of sedges or water-lilies close to the bank. If you should choose such a spot it is always worth trying the close water first, particularly for roach, but generally speaking the fish are well out in the stream and fishing between one-third and halfway across the river will bring the best results.

In fishing any swim the choice of float will depend upon a number of variables: the prevailing conditions of wind and stream, the weight of line and distance you wish to cast, and, of course, the actual manner in which you intend to search out your swim. Another factor I take into account when tackling up is one which I rarely hear mentioned by other anglers and that is what I have called 'float stability'. When trotting down on the Thames (on other rivers too, I am sure) it is sometimes essential (mostly always, as I shall explain later!) that the bait should precede the float and the remainder of the terminal tackle. This usually requires that you are continuously busy 'mending line', particularly if the length of cast from float to hook is greater than the depth of water. It is irritating to the angler and, I believe, off-putting to the fish, if every time an effort to mend line is made, it results in the float being pulled flat on to the surface of the water or dragged away from its natural path of descent downstream. (Imagine what is happening to the bait in such a situation . . .). A long rod combined with a light and buoyant line helps to make the mending of line easier, but a stable float is the important factor. To achieve this stability I use either a long slim float, a dual bodied float which I make

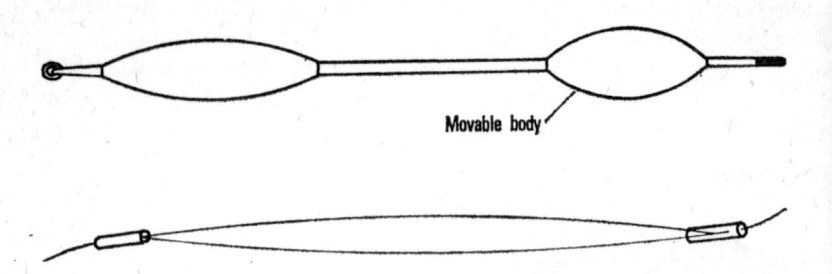

Fig. 1. Twin Bodied Float. Stem of cane or beech dowel, bodies of balsa, cork or elder pith. Method of attaching float to the line with valve tubing. This avoids tangles when casting and speeds up float changing.

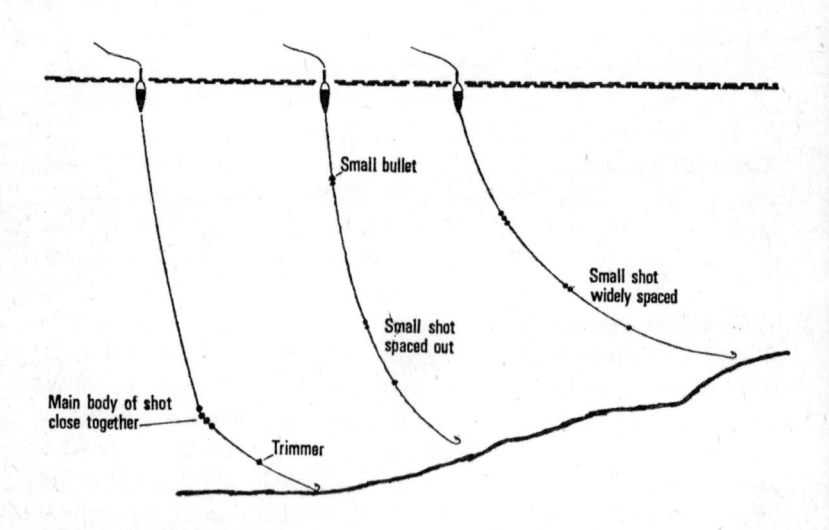

Fig. 2. (*L to R*) Getting the bait down quickly to fish on or close to the bottom. Bullet set to give casting weight and stability—slow sinking bait. 'Creeping' up a shelf or over an obstacle.

myself, or one of the 'fluted' Avon type floats invented, I believe, by Albert Smalley. These latter are very simply constructed from elder piths or balsa wood and the extra surface area they offer is a great assistance in obtaining extra 'grip' on the water.

By shotting the float well down in the water little bite sensitivity is lost, whilst the resistance of the water to the submerged body of the float enables you to mend line without unduly disturbing its equilibrium. Incidentally, the dual-bodied float I mentioned consists of two streamlined cork or balsa bodies on a long, thin quill or piece of cane. One body is fixed on the bottom of the cane, the other is moveable and is used as a stabiliser. The float is useful either as an antennae float for still water fishing, or as a stable float for long trotting. (Fig. 1).

For mid-stream fishing I usually choose a float which will carry between four and six bb shot, or a half inch barrel lead stopped by one shot. Under normal conditions this makes casting easy on the rod and easy on the angler. Should conditions demand it (a facing wind for example) I am never afraid to add more shot and use a larger float. Quick and accurate casting means that your bait spends more time on the vicinity of the fish—of great importance in match fishing, and yet I often watched anglers, particularly in matches, wasting their energy and tempting their patience by trying to pelt light tackle into the teeth of a wind simply because they were afraid of adding one or two more shots.

The actual positions of the shot on the line again depends upon prevailing conditions. Sometimes a slow sinking bait will take fish, but on the Thames, particularly if you are fishing a small bait, it will more often than not be bleak. I would say that for at least ninety per cent of the time, presentation of the bait on, and just off the bottom, will take most quality fish.

The method I find most effective, provided there is a reasonable stream, is to have the float set between six and eighteen inches deeper than the swim with the lowest shot 'knocking on' or just off the bottom. In fact, this lowest shot which I call the 'trimmer', is most important. I nip it on to the line very lightly so that I can move it at will and I experiment with it until I am satisfied my tackle is fishing as I want it to. (Fig. 2).

This method is not suitable for swimming down in very slack water. I find the best results are obtained by starting off with the float set just a few inches deeper than the swim and then moving it down little by little until I can get a smooth trot down without too many 'false-knocks' from the bait touching bottom.

Undoubtedly, fishing on or very close to the bottom is a very effective method for all species and many times, fishing in this way, I have had mixed bags of roach, barbel, chub and bream. I hinted earlier that it is not always necessary for the bait to preceed the float and, in fact, I quite often deliberately fish the other way round, with float dragging the bait down behind it. To the eye of the Trent purist it looks simply awful. I well remember the first time I fished the Thames with Jim Sharp and he saw me fishing what he referred to as 'this crude method', but there are times when it is positively killing, so give it a try.

The general positioning of the shot on the cast also depends very much upon the conditions of the day. I am not at all worried by having shot within a few inches of my hook, and I am quite convinced that the fish do not mind either. On the whole, I prefer my shot to be grouped together in one bunch rather than strung out. I bite them on gently so that on a not-too-fragile line they can be moved up or down at will. Generally speaking, the faster the water the greater the concentration of shot close to the hook, but other factors may require a different arrangement. For example, a ledge halfway down the swim may require 'creeping up', a process which can be quite simple with the correct arrangement of shot. In summer one may be faced with little stream, but the necessity for a long cast requires a fair amount of shot. This need can be met by setting a small running lead, or swan shot, a foot or two under the float to give casting power and stability, whilst the remaining shot can be arranged to give a slowly descending bait, or whatever may be required.

Contrary to popular belief, you will often catch more fish by moving your shot closer to the bait when fish are biting shyly as the bite will be signalled more quickly. In fast water I favour placing the main weight of shot three to four feet above the hook, perhaps two or three bb one foot to eighteen inches above the hook and the trimmer somewhere below them.

The main thing to remember is that the whole aim summed up in that mysterious word 'presentation' is to get the bait to the fish without arousing its suspicions. I do not believe for a

A nice pike

148½ lbs of bream (best fish 7¼ lb) taken in 4 hours fishing at Oxford—I believe that this is still a record catch

Netting a bream on a Thames backwater

Legering

The famous swim at Donnington Bridge

Match in progress—'H' section in the 1967 Thames Championship

A barbel from the Thames at Tadpole

Mixed bag

A 7 lb bream—Medley, Oxford

moment that fish count the number of shot or discriminate between a 2 lb. line and a 4 lb. line BUT, they will have little to do with a bait that behaves in an unnatural manner.

So far, I have been concerned with what might be called distance fishing; fishing well out in the stream, and trotting down. There are, however, times when heavy floats and shotting arrangements are unnecessary and, in fact, their use would be a serious handicap. Roach in particular have days of shyness, days when they can only be taken consistently on light tackle. The cool of summer evenings when the stream is very low often provides ideal conditions for the use of a cork-on-crow quill, single shot and eighteen hook. At such times the Thames takes on a tranquil, canal-like appearance and the use of ultra-light tackle brings fish to the net and aesthetic pleasure to the angler.

In winter too, I have found the need to change from medium to very light tackle when fishing eddies or slack water. Once when fishing for bream with Peter Tombleson we chose a piece of slack water in a very large eddy, noted for its flood-water fishing. We soon found that although the bream declined to feed, we were taking the odd sizeable roach. More often than not however, we discovered that our maggots had been 'got at' without the slightest indication of a bite showing on the float. Changing over to very light tackle we soon began to have bite after bite and finished up with 20 lb. each of prime Thames roach. I am sure that the reason is easy to appreciate. The conditions were very cold, the fish were congregated into a relatively small patch of water, the result was that although prepared to feed gently, they were not prepared to move far; thus the bites could only show on very finely balanced tackle.

3. Legering and Bite Detection

LEGERING, in one of its forms, is a highly popular and sometimes quite deadly method of fishing the Thames, being an ideal method of presenting a bait 'on the bottom' and at distance. There are, of course, numerous ways of tackling the subject and, in a treatment as short as this, there will be much that is left out, but I have caught a lot of fish on leger tackle and can claim easy acquaintanceship with all of the methods I describe.

Most leger techniques are in some way an adaptation of the straightforward running lead. I say straightforward, but of course, even the simple drilled bullet can be used in a variety of ways. Readers of angling papers and periodicals will be aware of the mystique and controversy surrounding such details as length of trail, methods of stopping the lead, type of lead to be used, and so on . . .

Although I shall be describing various types of leger tackle (and some refinements do offer real advantage under particular conditions) my own feeling is that the plain drilled bullet or Arlsey Bomb, attached directly to the line, is a method less complicated than many and as deadly as most.

The tendency of many anglers is to use the lightest lead with which they can hold bottom for a given flow of stream. This seems to me little more than a casual rule of thumb; an application of the 'lightest possible' rule, whereas in practice there may be one of several factors which leads the experienced leger man to choose one weight of lead rather than another.

On the whole I tend to use a heavier lead than most—perhaps choosing a $\frac{1}{2}$ oz. lead where a $\frac{1}{4}$ oz. lead would hold comfortably. The main reason for this is that I believe fish are easily put off if they feel the lead on the line. The equilibrium of a lead just holding bottom is easily disturbed. The fish may mouth the bait quite gently and then literally start the ball rolling. The stream will take over and the lead will bounce across the river bottom disturbing the fish, jerking the line, and giving a series of false-knocks. The heavier lead will hold bottom and is less likely to be disturbed as the fish picks up the bait, drawing line through it and transmitting the signal to the bite register. Another important consideration is the fact that I often very (particularly when legering for bream) have to cast considerable distances to the hot spot, sometimes in adverse wind conditions. The heavier lead not only makes it easier to cast long distances accurately, it helps me to keep in closer contact with my terminal tackle.

The distance between lead and hook (length of trail) will depend mainly upon the conditions of the river bed and the way in which the fish are feeding. When fishing amongst long, trailing weeds it is obvious that a long trail will be necessary to prevent the bait being pulled down amongst them and, on rivers like the Hampshire Avon, it is not unusual to see anglers fishing a trail of five feet or more. It must be remembered however that the longer the trail, the further a fish may move after taking the bait without indicating a bite!

Theoretically, a fish can move twice the length of the trail with the bait in its mouth without showing a positive knock. Under normal conditions, fishing a reasonably clean river bed, I tend to use a trail of from twelve to eighteen inches. If the fish are biting shyly I alter my length of trail and weight of lead until I find a combination which gives a positive indication of a taking fish. On a still day when I wish to make as little disturbance as possible with my casting and when I am reading bites on a slack line, I will possible choose a light lead fished two and a half or three feet from the bait. The length of trail here means that even if the lead does move it is so far from the bait that it will be unlikely to alarm the fish. On the other hand, missed bites on a wild, blustery day might persuade me to fish a heavy lead with a trail of only three to four inches. I should probably hold my line (possibly with the rod tip sunk beneath the surface of the water) and strike at every unusual twitch . . .

Methods of 'stopping the lead' i.e. preventing it from sliding down the line to the hook, are numerous. They range from pieces of matchstick and valve rubber to split-rings, glass beads, and of course, the ubiquitous split shot. My own feeling is that provided the hole in the leger weight is not too large, and the leger itself is not too heavy, the split shot works as well as anything, I don't believe for a moment that its slight weight in anyway deters a taking fish. It is important to ensure that the shot is firmly attached to the line and, in fact, I often use two as an insurance against one coming adrift or sliding down the line. In his book, *Still-Water Angling*, Dick Walker tells the story of losing a very large tench due to the shot on his line coming unstuck and allowing the leger to drop down on to the hook, neatly removing it from the fish's mouth. I thought it was rather a tall story until it happened to me!

Unless I am legering with a very small bait I invariably tie my hooks directly to the reel line. Occasionally when fishing a very snag-ridden swim I use a trail of a lower breaking strain than the reel-line to minimise the loss of leger weights but, even so, find that it is usually the leger rather than the hook which becomes caught up and lose it anyway. I rarely leger with a line of less than three pounds as a light line offers little real advantage and it is very easy to break on the strike when legering for large fish a long way off.

A very simple and effective rig is the link-leger. There are many variations but the two I commonly use are easily made up. (Fig. 3). The first consists simply of a length of nylon line (say six to nine inches) attached to a small brass split ring. The reel line is passed through the ring in the usual way and stopped at the required distance from the hook. On the nylon (which forms the link) you may either tie something like an Arlsey Bomb, or (cheaper!) a paternoster lead, or you can squeeze on some large split shot. The latter are cheap and offer the advantage of an easily adjustable weight. The second method looks somewhat cruder but is simpler, and if anything, even more effective. For this, all that is required is a piece of nylon doubled to form a loop and joined together by nipping a split shot over both strands. One shot must be close enough to the end of the loop to form an 'eye' which takes the place of the split ring; other weight may be added as required. (Fig. 4).

The whole idea of the link-leger arrangement is to avoid friction as far as possible; the only resistance to a taking fish is the rod tip or bite indicator, or the float if one is used. On this tackle one often finds that fish take with complete confidence; bites are often indicated by a gentle curving of the rod. Its great advantage is that fish can move the bait without drawing line through the split ring and yet still register a bite. In fact,

SIMPLE 'LOOP LEGER'

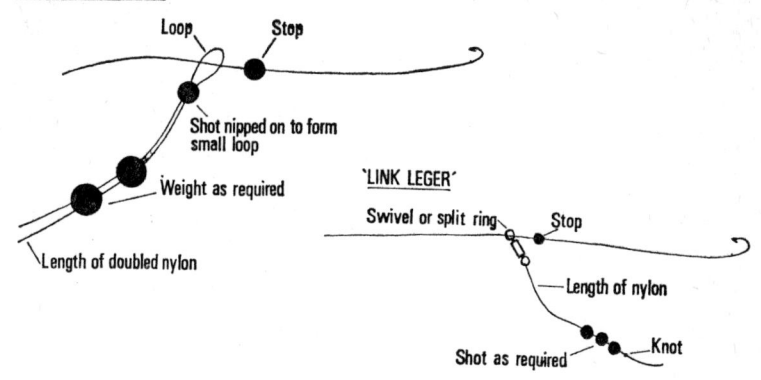

Fig. 4. Simple 'Loop Leger'.

Fig. 3. 'Link Leger'.

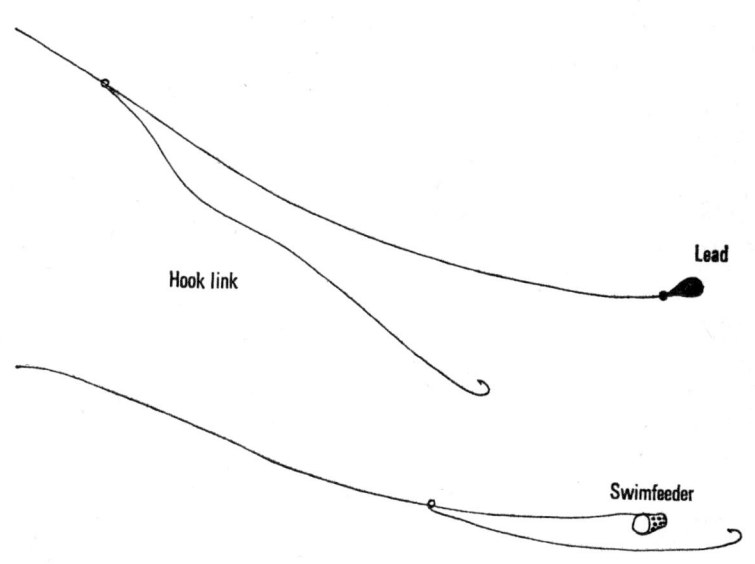

Fig. 5. Paternoster—The hook link may be running or fixed and set at any required distance from the lead.

Fig. 6. The swim-feeder may be fished paternoster style with the hook in the baited area.

provided that the link is long enough, I doubt whether it needs to be a running leger at all.

One slight adaptation I favour is the use of a clip swivel in place of the split ring. It is easily stopped by a small split shot and makes for an easy change of weight.

These, then, are the basic rigs for the running leger though, of course, there are many types of lead available, some of them specifically designed for use under particular conditions such as the 'Capta' lead, so designed that its shape helps it to hold bottom in fast water, or the old fashioned coffin lead with its flat surface which helps to prevent it sinking into a muddy bottom.

There is another method in which a fixed lead is used, sometimes called a paternoster, though that term is more accurately used to describe the live-baiting rig we use for perch. It is particularly useful for fishing a bait above weed, or for keeping the bait away from a muddy or foul bottom. In appearance it is rather like a link-leger except that the lead is attached to the bottom of the reel line and the bait is suspended from the bottom. (Fig. 5). The bite from a fish is communicated directly through the reel line and, without any intermediary swivel or lead, it can be very sensitive. It is very useful for fishing mid-water in conditions which rule out the use of conventional float tackle.

The last item of terminal tackle I wish to mention is the swim-feeder. Swim-feeders are very popular amongst Thames anglers and there is no doubt that they have proved their worth under some conditions. Many anglers design and make their own, wire and perspex being the most usual materials, and I know one angler who does very well with a certain brand of ladies hair curler only very slightly adapted to fit on to the line. They can, however, be bought from tackle dealers and it is this commercial pattern which I shall describe.

Basically, the swim-feeder is a tube of perspex open at both ends and weighted with a strip of lead. The weight of the lead may be varied for different conditions of stream. As its name implies, the swim-feeder is used to introduce groundbait into the vicinity of the baited hook. The groundbait is packed into the cylinder, the feeder is cast to the appropriate spot, then the action of the stream washes the groundbait from the cylinder and so spreads an invitation to the feast close to the baited hook.

Where there is little stream a quantity of dry groundbait should be packed in the centre of the cylinder. The water will cause this to expand, forcing the contents out of the feeder into the swim. The feeder may also be packed with maggots provided that each end is firmly sealed with solid groundbait to prevent them being deposited in flight. (Fig. 6).

The most popular way of attaching the swim-feeder is rather after the fashion of the link-leger and it can be used with either a fixed or a running link.

The swim-feeder enthusiasts claim that the method enables them to place an economical amount of groundbait in just the place it will do most good, i.e. in close proximity to the baited hook and undoubtedly it does this. Personally, however, I rarely use them. From the point of view of groundbaiting they are useful only when relatively small amounts of groundbait are to be used, or where one is unsure of the distribution of groundbait thrown into the stream in the normal manner. I sometimes use them for searching out bream swims where I am reluctant to 'invest' in large quantities of groundbait before I am sure I am on to the fish, but even then, I reckon that in normal conditions I can spread my invitation by hand and then cast accurately on to it.

To use swim-feeders indiscriminately as I have seen them used, for example, on narrow streams where the flow of water has been negligible, or on still waters, seems to me absolutely pointless.

One obvious disadvantage is that one must either use a powerful rod to suit them and thus lose a great deal of sensitivity, or face the fact that their use with a light rod must eventually ruin it. The strain involved in casting one any distance at all is considerable.

There have been numerous different approaches to solving the problem of bite detection when legering and I am sure that more will appear, for the minds of anglers are notoriously inventive. The most simple method of all is, of course, watching the rod tip, and under many conditions I find it the most satisfactory. When, for instance, the bream are 'well on', there is little difficulty in seeing knocks, the bites being signalled by a good solid tug on the rod-tip. In fact, nearly all species, when they get down to really serious feeding, will give ample indication they are interested in your bait, and it does not take a vast amount of skill to hook them. Unfortunately (perhaps?) on most days you will find the fish feeding moderately or gently, bites are less obvious and it is consequently more difficult to connect.

To be effective, tight-line legering requires constant concentration and quick reflexes; it is not a method for the lazy angler. One of its great attractions is its simplicity of form and technique. After casting, the reel is turned sufficiently to tighten up the line and the rod may either be held or placed in the rod-rest or rests. Personally, I hate holding the rod if I am using the rod tip as my bite indicator. I find that no matter how still I am there is always some dithering of the rod tip which makes it difficult to detect shy bites. I prefer to use one or two rests, depending upon the position I want the rod, and then to sit with my hands cupped around but not actually touching the butt. In calm conditions I like the rod set at an angle of about thirty degrees so that when I am crouched forward ready for the strike the tip is just about level with my eyes. In blustery conditions when I am relying upon some form of indicator, or perhaps, feeling for bites on the line, I have the tip close to, or even immersed in, the water.

The great problem which always faces the leger angler is resistance and, even when this has been largely overcome in the arrangement of the terminal tackle, there is still the problem of the fish feeling the resistance at the rod tip. Provided the bait is presented in such a way as to overcome the suspicions of the fish, and the fish are feeding confidently, then most fish, and particularly the larger species, give sufficient warning to enable even a man with slow reflexes to strike and connect. The fact is, however, that very often the fish are feeding shyly. Most anglers will have experienced occasions when, time after time, on retrieving the tackle it is found that the bait has been 'got at' without there being any indication of a bite. I have quite often taken good fish consistently when anglers sitting around me have seen no indication of a bite and have, in fact, accused me of striking indiscriminately. It is really quite amazing how large fish—bream of 4-5 lb. for example—can take a bait so delicately. I am often asked about timing a strike, but the only answer I can give is 'strike when the hook is in the fish's mouth'; and it is up to you to know when.

It was discussion of these types of problems in the Oxford

Specimen Hunters Group which led Peter Stone to design his now famous 'Ledgerstrike' (he spells 'ledger' differently to me!) which incorporates an extremely fine tip. It has proved very successful, being very delicate and light to handle it is a most sensitive tool. For my part I don't go much on the usual run of rods designed for legering as I think they are usually too short. My own preference is for a rod (which I mentioned earlier) originally called the Peter Tombleson Float Rod which *Angling Times* kindly gave me for catching rather a lot of bream on one occasion. It is a very soft actioned rod, twelve feet three inches long, built cane, made by James and I find it indicates the most delicate of bites. In very windy weather it tends to flop about rather so then I change to my old Apollo, another rod which has done sterling service over the years. It seems to me that a longer rod must, as a simple matter of mechanics, lead to a quicker strike, but the important factor, I suppose, is to fish with a rod you know and feel happy to use. You should aim at reading your rod tip as a float fisherman reads his float.

So far, I have been concerned only with tight line legering, but when fishing slack water in reasonably still conditions I very often fish with a slack line and watch the bow in the line, instead of the rod tip, for bite indication. It can be a very deadly method, for the fish feels very little resistance indeed, and one soon learns to interpret the movement of the line.

A hint worth mentioning here is something that I once saw described in Sheringham's *Coarse Fishing*, as 'easing the fish'. Quite early on in my angling career I found that one would sometimes have real, thumping bites, but find them extremely difficult to hit. Sometimes these are caused by gudgeon, or rather small fish, tugging at the bait (a gudgeon can move a rod tip in such a way as to suggest at least an 8 lb. bream or 10 lb. barbel)! but at other times these bites indicate the intentions of an interested but suspicious fish of larger proportions. The drill is to give slack line at the first twitching indication of a bite and take hold of the line just above the reel. The first movements of the fish are felt as very gentle twitches or tugs—almost as though someone is sandpapering the line—and you will feel a little line being drawn through your fingers. The lack of resistance seems to give the fish confidence and a slow steady pull develops. That is the time to strike!

Of course, all manner of means have been used to overcome

resistance in indicating bites and new ideas are constantly coming up. The dough-bobbin is the original of many, that is, a piece of bread paste or dough squeezed on to the line, usually between the butt-ring and reel. It forms an angle in the line which straightens out to signal a bite. More sophisticated versions of the same principle have been constructed with corks, sticks and table-tennis balls, to name but a few materials. Those which appeal to me most are those which require least setting up after each cast. I enjoy experimenting with new ideas and have tried all manner of bite indicators.

One of the first I used and found to be successful was what has been described as an ariel float. (Fig. 7.) This consists of a piece of cork or balsa wood, drilled through the centre to take either a piece of hollow quill or the empty tube of a ball pen, and shaped to fit like a plug into the butt ring of the rod. I fit all of my rods with the large, stainless steel butt rings one normally sees on spinning rods and which are designed for use with the fixed spool reel. When setting up your tackle the float is threaded on the line between the butt and the second ring. For casting, the float is plugged into the butt ring and the cast is made through it. After the cast is made you pop it out on to the line where it functions like the conventional dough bobbin. The floats can be weighted to suit prevailing condition of stream.

The butt indicator works on a similar principle really, though it looks quite different. It is simply a short lever with a split eye at one end and a hinge which clips on to the butt at the other. The reel line is passed through the eye and, as with the dough bobbin, an angle is formed in the line. (Fig. 8). The hinge is sometimes adjustable to allow for differences in the force of the stream and I have seen this type of indicator adapted to fit on the top joint rather than on the butt.

The latter is rather an important point. I tend to refer to indicators which are fished 'inside' or 'outside' of the rod, and I prefer the latter. It seems obvious to me that the closer the indicator is to the bait the more sensitive it will be. Another point is that I see most 'inside' indicators fished on a rod which is propped at an angle to the water which drastically cuts down on their efficiency. I long ago discovered that when finger-tip legering (i.e. holding the line) if I held my rod up thus forming an angle between line and rod, the friction (resistance) was so great at the rod tip that I would always *see* a slight movement

LEGERING AND BITE DETECTION   43

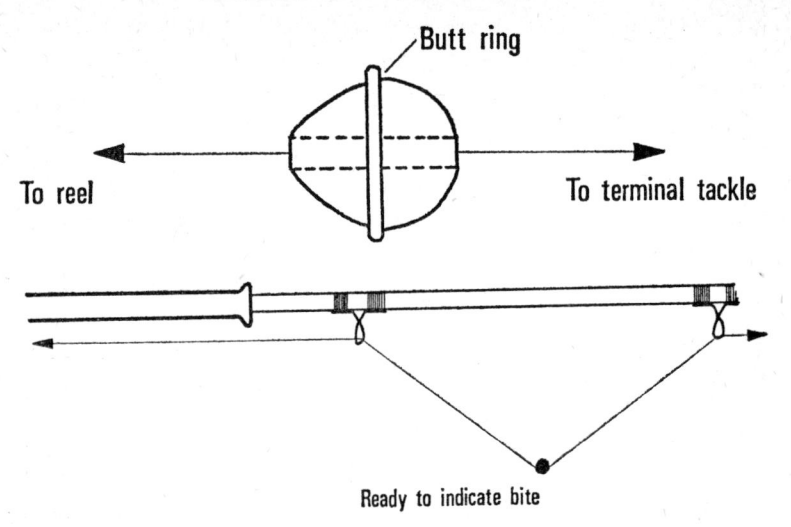

To reel → Butt ring → To terminal tackle

Ready to indicate bite

FIG. 7. The Ariel Float
Float plugged into ring ready for casting.

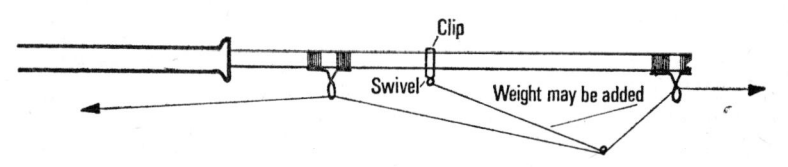

Clip
Swivel Weight may be added

FIG. 8. A simple bite indicator—these are sometimes clipped to the top joint of the rod.

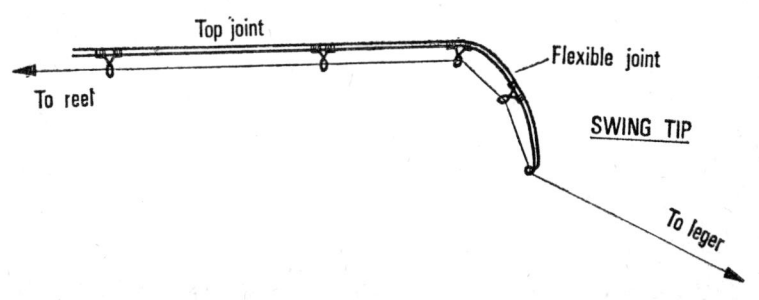

Top joint
To reel
Flexible joint
SWING TIP
To leger

FIG. 9. The swing tip bite indicator

before I *felt* a bite. In other words, when finger-tip legering or using an 'inside' indicator, the more neatly you can have your rod 'pointing down the line' as it were, the more delicate will be your bite registration.

One of the most controversial bite indicators of its day was the swing tip, (Fig. 9). I am not quite sure why it was so controversial except that it is in the nature of anglers to be conservative. The funny thing was that the tip was slated by many anglers who were leger-men and yet was taken up by match anglers who, until its inception, never thought of using leger tackle at all. That it was successful is convincingly proved by the many match wins it has yielded.

I could never understand why it was considered to be so controversial. Clayton of Boston, its inventor, kindly sent me one and I found it very effective. In a sense it was a very logical development in legering as it combined something of the principles of the ultra-fine tip with that of the dough bobbin fished 'outside'. Simple, but in its way quite brilliant and Mr. Clayton deserves full praise.

Basically, it consists of a piece of pliable plastic carrying two rod rings (one intermediate, one end ring) and it is whipped or otherwise fitted to the rods top joint. It can also be purchased as an integral part of a fibre-glass top joint, the ferrule of which can be shaped to fit any conventional rod.

When setting up, the line is passed through the rod and the swing tip rings so that the swing tip virtually becomes an extension of the rod except that it plays no part in the actual playing of the fish.

After casting and allowing the leger to settle in the desired position, the slack line between swing tip and leger is taken in until the tip is hanging at about right angles to the reel line. In fact, like the 'outside' dough bobbin, it makes an angle in the line which is straightened out when a fish takes the bait. In this case it is signalled by the tip rising. Differing conditions can be allowed for by wrapping lead wire around the tip.

Lastly, in this section, I should like to mention the use of the conventional float with leger tackle. To my mind there is no more sensitive bite indicator than a well shotted float. The trouble with float legering is that, except in still waters, the float which is sufficiently buoyant to overcome vagaries of wind and stream is often too buoyant to act as a really sensitive bite detector.

When fishing a fairly shallow stretch with not too much stream it is possible to use a float attached to the line in the normal way. When conditions permit the use of a float, I use the lightest possible, attached by the bottom ring only and so set that it is half-cocked when the line is tightened up. With this method I strike at the slightest movement of the float. For deeper water I favour a fairly large slider (sliders *must* be pretty bouyant otherwise they don't slide) stopped by a small piece of nylon. Unfortunately, most commercially produced sliders are fitted with rings so large that the size of the stop required interferes with smooth casting, the only suitable sliders I have seen are designed by Billy Lane.

A method I favour a great deal on the Thames is what I call a 'free float'—it is a method somewhat similar to what the midlanders call bobbing but it has certain important differences. Its great advantage is that it allows the use of a float in streams which would pull a normal float below the surface if they were tethered to a fixed leger. The rig is shown in Fig. 10 and the method of fishing it in Fig. 11. The line is passed through the bottom ring of the float but no stop is used on the line above the float (hence 'free float'). After casting, the float will sometimes (but not always) disappear below the surface. Until you know the stream, allow the float to reappear before tightening up the line and then tighten up a little at a time until the float is lying in its angle, comfortably riding the stream. The nearer you can keep it to the terminal tackle the better; generally speaking, the stronger the stream the more it will work its way towards you.

Incidentally, in choosing a float I have a decided preference for a medium sized 'Thames Slim' when fishing this method. It needs to have a smooth wire ring at the bottom and if there is not too much stream running its sensitivity can be increased by wrapping a turn or two of lead wire around its stem.

A bite may be signalled in any one of many ways; the float is 'sitting' at an angle on the line, how acute that angle is (mainly dependent upon the stream) will affect the type of bite indication shown. If the angle is fairly acute a bite will be signalled by a straightforward pull down but more often you will see a dip or a bob, or even the float moving up against the

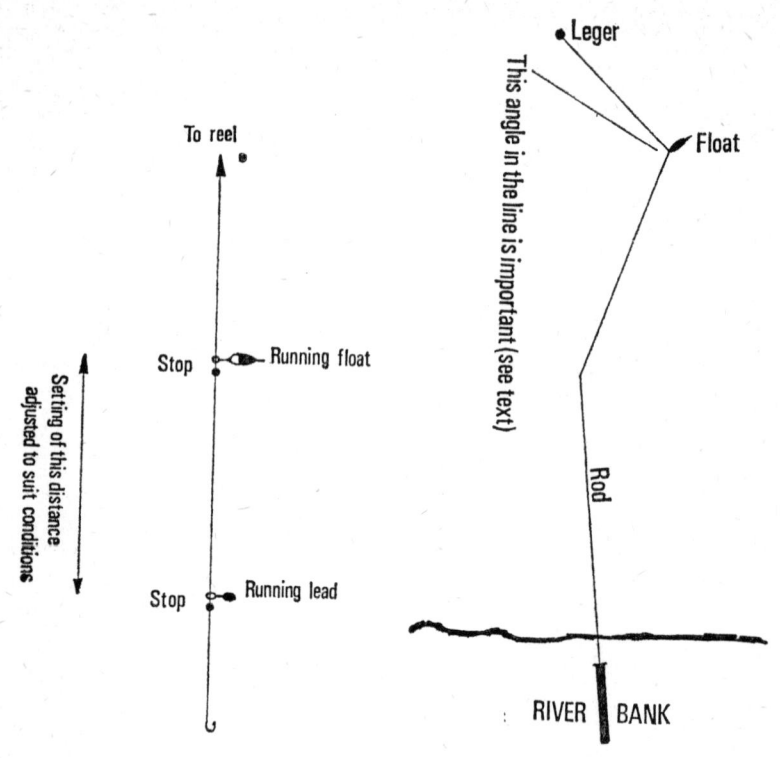

FIG. 10. Setting up free float tackle.
FIG. 11. Fishing the free float.

stream. The great advantage of this method is that it can be adapted for use in a wide range of conditions and with practice it can be adjusted to a really terrific degree of sensitivity. I have had some splendid bags of bream fishing this way and somehow I find a float to watch most enjoyable and less tiring for the eyes.

It sounds more technical than it is but a few important points are worth remembering when tackling up. The float ring must be large enough to allow the float to rise easily up the line, but not too large. If the ring is small the float remains trapped beneath the surface of the water; if it is too large you will find that when you cast the float remains at your rod tip as the leger flies out into the blue.

I have also found in casting that the distance the float travels with the terminal tackle is related to the distance between the leger weight and the stop for the float. If you find that the float suddenly stops in mid air whilst the leger continues on its way, try moving the float stop down on the line.

I am very fond of this method and have described it in detail because I consider it to be one of the most killing methods I know; in fact *the* killing method on its day.

4. Match Fishing the Thames

THE REAL home of match fishing is the Midlands, but though the upper Thames is within fairly easy reach of the big match fishing centres, it is not very popular as a match river because of the strict enforcement of the Thames Conservancy size limit. With the notable exception of the Thames Championships which embrace all Thames-side clubs, most of the matches tend to be local affairs and most of them are fished by Thames anglers.

The northern and midland teams tend to look upon southern match anglers as easy meat: and not without reason. The competition in Thames matches is not nearly as fierce as it is amongst the midlanders: bookmakers are virtually unkown and it is by no means all of the matches which sport even a modest sweep. On the odd occasions when the midland teams do come down to fish against the Thames locals they are often the victors and compare with Thames matchmen as professionals compare with amateurs. And in a sense they are. To be fair to

the average Thames angler, he does not want to be involved in the cut and thrust of competitive angling. He has an excellent river to fish, enjoys fishing it, and looks upon the occasional match as something of a lark. He is the pleasure angler by tradition whereas the midland angler is very often a match angler first and foremost—in fact, many of the waters he fishes would be of very little interest unless there was organised competitive fishing.

The main reason for the low standard of Thames match fishing is, I believe, the Thames size limit rule. For one thing, it keeps away the majority of match anglers who will only fish 'all-in' matches, for another, it encourages the belief prevalent among Thames anglers, that 'match tactics' as they are known elsewhere, do not pay off on the Thames.

The size limit was designed primarily to prevent people from taking away undersized fish, but in these days of keepnets, it is doubtful whether it serves any real purpose. The usual argument that it prevents immature fish from being damaged in keepnets does not hold water at all; it is surely true that large fish are more likely to suffer injury in a net than small ones. It would seem much more sensible to increase the minimum size for keepnets and to disallow the common practice of carrying fish to a central point for the weigh-in.

Still, I am speaking only as an individual and though I do not think that the feeling is as strong as it was a few years ago, it does appear that most Thames anglers are in favour of the size rule.

I have said that the Thames size rule is the main reason for the generally poor standard of match fishing and I am quite sure it has had the effect of slowing down the adoption of modern match fishing techniques. The common attitude on the Thames is that midland style match fishing is only suitable for tiddler snatching. On the upper Thames, I would say bread in one of its forms is the most commonly used bait—'You get too much small stuff on maggots'. Legering or laying-on are favoured methods as it is widely thought that they bring the bigger fish ... 'and anyway, swimming the stream is too much like hard work.'

This attitude does tend to encourage the mediocre. True, a large piece of breadpaste will usually produce a large fish—when it produces anything at all. Hence the complacent angler sitting on his basket contemplating his motionless float. 'Ah!' he says, 'They're off today.'

Having banned gudgeon, bleak, pike and eels, and having set minimum sizes for all of the other species, he is mainly concerned that his luck should be in. Of course, there are some Thames anglers who would like to go further and ban groundbait, and I have heard numerous arguments in favour of barring bream. (Why not barbel or chub or, for that matter, roach and dace?).

If we think of the upper Thames as a match river we must be prepared to think in pretty large terms. It is a wide river for much of its length, and fairly deep; it contains a good head of large fish of various species which are quite widely spread. Roach are numerous and of a good average size, pounders being reasonably common. Bream are present in ever increasing numbers (in fact I should rate the upper Thames as one of the best bream rivers in the country) and if you are fishing a breamy stretch they are likely to be the match winners. In fact in the Oxford area it often needs something like 70 to 100 lb. to win a match! Dace are sometimes present in large shoals and can be useful match fish, whilst chub and barbel are likely to turn up anywhere and the latter, in particular, are often tackle breakers.

I had a good deal to say about tackle in my earlier chapter, much of which applies to match fishing. A fixed spool reel and a rod which will comfortably pelt your tackle out into the middle of a sixty yard stretch wide are an absolute necessity.

If the match rules allow competitors to set up two outfits, I strongly recommend it. I usually have one rod set up with float tackle on about $2\frac{1}{2}$ lb. line and another equipped with 4 to 6 lb. line and leger tackle.

My usual routine is to commence fishing with a smallish bait fished close to or 'knocking-on' the bottom. This is an excellent method for the better class roach and if the bream, barbel or chub are present they will usually let you know quite quickly. By this method too, the swim can be explored for depth, proximity of weed beds etc., and the information added to that already received from discreet use of the plummet.

Should the larger species show themselves, then lose no time in bringing the heavy tackle into play. Nothing is more frustrating than to be broken by a big fish which would count for so much in a match. Having a second set of tackle ready saves that maddening business of tackling up with trembling fingers, cursing every wasted moment. It saves time and trouble and encourages you to change methods if fishing is slack. Even when the bigger fish are not evident, they can sometimes be picked up on leger tackle when they will not look at a bait offered on float tackle.

On most stretches of the Thames the bream are not sufficiently predominant to fish for them exclusively, unless you are drawn in a known bream swim or should happen to see them moving. Even on the well known bream stretches the fishing is patchy—the shoals are often huge, but they do move around a great deal.

I usually start by roach fishing well out in the stream. I always fish hard on the bottom, and if there is sufficient stream to keep my bait well ahead of my shot distribution I like to fish with the distance between float and hook about twelve inches greater than the depth of the water.

Unless the fish are located in one particular part of the swim, it pays to fish out the whole length before retrieving for the next cast. It frequently happens that when, for example, roach are being taken half way down a swim, a trot down of a further five or six yards will produce chub or bream. Many anglers adopt the policy of baiting up two swims, one well out in the stream and one closer to the bank. As well as offering an alternative if one swim should need resting, it can be very useful if the wind changes during the course of a match and so makes the control of tackle difficult when fishing at a distance.

If the bream are about it will pay to change to a line of at least 5 to 6 lb. and, although they can quite often be taken on float tackle, it is usually found that the leger is quicker and deadlier. Although one tends to think of match fishing in terms of light tackle, I recommend a fairly heavy line—even 6 or 7 lb. is not out of the way—when faced with a shoal of Thames bream which are really 'on'. The main requirement is, of course, that you should be able to bring the fish to net with the minimum waste of time and disturbance of the swim.

On many of the well known match rivers the bream are small, averaging perhaps a pound or so; the occasional $3\frac{1}{2}$-pounder comes as rather a nuisance. On the Thames the bream are large, a shoal might easily average $4\frac{1}{2}$ lb. with the odd fish going well over 5 lb. You cannot waste time playing these chaps on 2 lb. line. As a bream must be at least twelve inches to 'weigh', the 'skimmers', or what one hears referred to as 'nice match fish' on midland rivers, are to be avoided.

Provided you have the skill to handle your tackle in such a way as to present an unsuspicious looking bait at a distance of twenty to thirty yards, then the next major point is that of baits and groundbaits.

First of all, baits. Perhaps the maggot may fairly be called the universal match bait and there is no doubt in my mind that it takes a lot of beating, provided it is fished properly. It will certainly take any fish from the lofty carp to the lowly gudgeon. So will other baits, worm or bread, or possibly wheat, but they do not possess the other advantages of maggots. For various reasons maggots are looked down upon by big fish hunters. The general opinion is that you will not take the better class of fish on maggots, but I contest this most vigorously for I have proved, time and time again, that they can.

For all-round match fishing the maggot has many advantages: it is speedy to use, it stays on the hook well for long casting, it is not easily dragged off the hook when 'bumping bottom', it is an excellent attractor used either 'loose-feeding' or introduced into the swim via the cereal groundbait, singly, it offers a small bait or it can be fished in 'bunches'. Lastly, the fish like them. Its two main disadvantages are that it undoubtedly proves attractive to small fish and it is fairly expensive to use in large quantities.

This latter point has a great deal with its lack of popularity on the Thames. Where the prizes to be won in competition are meagre, the anglers are not so prepared to invest in baits and groundbaits. The anglers who claim that maggots are a waste of time, are usually those who turn up at a match equipped with a 'couple of bob's worth.' (I have actually heard this in a tackle shop: 'I'd better have a tanner's worth of maggots. I'm fishing in a match tomorrow.') Now, I am not in the maggot business, and I am not concerned with selling anglers more maggots, but the fact is that, generally speaking, a couple of shilling's worth of maggots is a waste of time. To really get the fish going on maggots you must feed them into your swim; even in summer conditions, with little stream running, I would say that something like a quart of maggots, at least, would be necessary for a match. In winter, with a stream running and the fish going well, a gallon would not be too many.

Of course, in summer, small fish are a nuisance, the pestilential bleak in particular. The only answer is to get rid of them by feeding lightly with surface feed and to ensure that your bait passes quickly through the 'bleak barrier'. I usually find however, that once the larger fish are in the swim and feeding, the bleak disperse.

Although I greatly favour maggots, there is no doubt that many anglers do very well on bread too. I prefer to fish it in the form of crust or flake and, with the latter, I have had some tremendous bags of bream. Crust is an excellent bait too, and I particularly like it for close, gentle swims when roach fishing. With this bait I invariably find that the bites, when they come, are bold and determined. Breadpaste I rarely use; in fact, almost all of my paste fishing is done with cheese paste which, though perhaps best known as a chub bait, seems to be equally popular with barbel, bream and roach. With cheese paste, it does not seem to matter how 'high' it is, but the softer the more effective. In fact I have heard Peter Stone's paste described as being 'like soup.'

I would say that most matches on the upper Thames are won with bags of bream and, although they are fish of catholic tastes, worm is undoubtedly the best bait. Lobworms are usually the easiest to obtain (with the aid of a discreetly shaded torch one can easily pick up a couple of hundred on a dark wet night) and again, to obtain the best results, you need sufficient to introduce a fair amount into the ground bait. During the last five years I lived in Oxford I took at least one bream bag of 100 lb. plus, and they were all taken on worm of one kind or another. The only really big catch I had on any other bait during that period was 97 lb., taken one November on maggot and float tackle. I eventually came to the conclusion that the best bait of all, at any time of the year (and on any bream water I have fished) is red worm—those little juicy chaps you find in compost and rotted grass-cuttings. Next in popularity I place lobworms, either fished whole or with the head nipped off, and thirdly, I would choose brandlings, though there are times when bream will completely disregard lobs and yet grab at any brandling you throw at them. Incidentally, one reads a great deal about 'maiden' lobs, a term used to describe a worm without an egg band: I do not think the egg band matters a great deal, but I do select the smaller, softer looking lobs for the hook and use the big rough ones for groundbait!

Hemp and wheat are not very popular baits on the upper Thames, in fact, the former is banned on a good many waters. I do not share in the general prejudice against it (it is all based upon 'old wives' tales, anyway) and consider it an excellent bait, particularly for roach. Creed wheat has enjoyed something of a revival in recent years. I first used it fishing the Oxford Canal with Billy Lane and some of the Coventry boys, and it was an eye-opener for me. On the Thames it very often takes some time to get the fish going on wheat, but once they are it is a killer. I have also found wheat very useful for baiting up swims in advance as it seems to gather and hold the fish much better than the usual bread mixes.

The preparation and use of groundbait is very much an art and its successful mastery will do much to place you in the top few in most matches.

In the first place, if you are fishing a stretch which is known to hold bream, you must prepare accordingly, in case you have the good fortune to get amongst them. This means that the amount of groundbait required is limited only by your capacity to carry it! It would be difficult to have too much when the fish are really on.

For bream fishing generally, it does not matter too much what form your groundbait takes. Because I do so much bream fishing, I try to produce my groundbait as cheaply as possible. For a good 'holding' mixture I use a base of well-soaked bread mixed with bran, chicken meal, sausage rusk, breadcrumbs or one of the proprietary brands of groundbait available from tackle shops. As I have an arrangement with a local baker who sells me stale bread by the sack-full it is not too expensive.

For match fishing, where one is competing against other anglers' offerings, I like to make my groundbait as attractive as possible and avoid the use of such stiffeners as bran, which darkens the mix. At one time I used to make my own breadcrumbs by slowly drying bread (I had access to a boiler room which did the job very well) and then pounding it up in a strong sack. It takes a lot of loaves for not very many breadcrumbs but they do swell tremendously in water so a little goes a long way. Now that I have less free time to devote to my angling preparation I tend to buy breadcrumbs by the hundredweight and, in that sort of quantity, they are not prohibitively expensive. Fine breadcrumbs make an excellent groundbait for any species; they can be mixed to make a gentle cloud, or to sink straight to the bottom of even a fast flowing swim; a ball will hold together well for throwing long distances and yet break up in the water to produce a tempting carpet; it can be used alone to attract, or mixed with bread to hold a shoal of feeding fish.

When using maggots or worms on the hook, I like to offer a liberal free sample in the groundbait. Of course, when roach fishing one has to take care not to overfeed, but when the fish are there in quantity it takes a large amount of food to keep them feeding in your swim on a large river like the Thames. The appetites of barbel and bream for lobworms can be quite enormous and I am happiest when I can afford a couple of hundred or so to chop up and mix with the groundbait.

Finally, I would bring the readers attention to the old adage that many matches are won well before the day. The keen angler leaves nothing undone in his preparation that could have any bearing on the outcome of the match. Of course, if you draw a really bad swim, much of your hard work will be in vain—on the other hand, should you draw a good stretch you can be confident of making the most of it.

Many anglers talk as though 'luck' is the all important factor in fishing: if I thought it was I would give it up and take to golf. Of course, in peg down matches the draw is important, and on the Thames perhaps more important than on many other rivers, but just watch how often the same names come up in match fishing circles. Take it from me, those boys make their own luck!

5. Choosing a Swim

THE THAMES has been kind to me; at least, it has amply rewarded the many hours I have devoted to learning something of its secrets. But it is not an easy river. I have fished with anglers in many parts of the country and often have my leg pulled about some of my big catches . . . 'It must be dead easy', they say, 'You wouldn't do that here'. Well, certainly, to catch large fish or huge quantities, it is pretty obvious that you must fish a water which can produce them and, I would say, from that angle the Thames is one of the best rivers in the country. But the fish still have to be caught, and that is a problem wherever you fish.

When this book was first published some years ago, one of the critics (most of them were very kind to me!) complained that it was supposed to be a book about the Thames but much of what I had to say could have been applied to any river. Not surprising when you think of it. In different parts and in different moods the Thames offers just about every type of coarse fishing that one can imagine. In the depths of summer you may find yourself using what are virtually still-water tactics—fishing the same swim in winter would approximate more to trotting down on the Avon.

The river varies considerably in width, but even the narrower stretches of the upper Thames offer a formidable amount of water to cover. I can tell you quite a lot about methods and tactics which have proved successful but, without doubt, the great problem is that of locating the fish. As I have said elsewhere, [*The Competent Angler*, A. & C. Black] I divide the business of catching fish into three parts: preparation; location; presentation, and it is the middle one which provides most of the difficulties. Once the fish have been located one can then worry about the most suitable method for getting them into the net. The Thames is a wonderful coarse fish river but it can be—and in fact generally is—very patchy. The fish are not spread about like cherries in a cake, they tend to be restricted to particular areas and they also tend to move around a lot.

In choosing a swim on any unfamiliar stretch of water we are guided by certain general rules. Generally speaking, we expect the fish to be in the shallows in summer and in the deeper water in winter, the proximity of reeds, sedges and underwater weed beds are related to the location of many species. We also use, almost unconsciously perhaps, our experience of other waters, other days. We 'like the look of a swim', a spot 'looks breamy' or we 'feel' that the fish should be in a certain place. In fact, with thought, we can greatly improve our facility for 'swim-spotting' by consciously thinking about what we are doing each time we visit the waterside. When you are catching fish don't just accept it as a lucky freak, try to figure out why... why are the fish in this particular swim?, are there any obvious reasons? could it be connected with temperature... light... speed of flow...?

Of course, on some rivers it is relatively easy to 'read the water'. Give me a swift flowing stream like the Swale and I will know just where to expect to pick up a trout lying in his sheltered spot behind a rock or stone, the head and tail of a glide will probably produce dace or grayling, whilst a slow pushing stretch beneath trees or a high bank is an obvious swim for chub. On the slow rivers (and I have seen the Thames devoid of flow even in winter) it is not so easy, and I have seen some of the country's top anglers stumped when it came to choosing a swim on a wide, slow stretch of the Thames at Oxford.

I should say that on the whole, the Thames is not a summer river; it is at its best from September onwards. On the other hand, huge bags of bream are taken during the summer months and I would rate the best bream hunting month as mid-July to mid-August. Unfortunately the problem of locating fish is in many ways much more difficult and particularly so in hot, dry summers when there is hardly any stream at all, when, as we say, 'the river is running backwards'.

In summer swim hunting, I tend to look for a spot either in a bay or on the inside of a bend fringed with sedges and in close proximity to weed and lily beds. There are many such places on the Thames, and although they can be a nuisance, I am always confident that if I am fishing over a lily-bed (or 'cabbage-patch' as we call them) the fish cannot be too far away. I also look out for reed mace, for where you see reed mace growing you can be pretty sure of a clean sandy or gravel bottom.

Incidentally, there are many little backwaters and cuts on the Thames which are often neglected by anglers. These are always worthwhile exploring for tench in the summer and pike in the winter. I have had fantastic sport from one of these backwaters where the area of fishable water was considerably less than the size of the average living room.

Most anglers, and I suppose I am one of them, prefer to choose a swim and then fish it out. They look with scorn upon the chap with a 'round-bottom' who cannot sit still for hours on end. I used to be like that. Once I had settled down in a swim and baited up I would wait all day in the hope that the fish would 'come on'. This is what I call the 'bream hole theory'.

During the summer I concentrate principally upon bream fishing as the roach fishing does not come into its best until much later in the year. The Thames is a fabulous bream river and has fished extraordinarily well in recent years. Some of the old-stagers reckon that this is due to some sort of magical influx of bream, but I do not believe that for a minute. The bream have been there long enough, people did not know how to fish for them! I remember when I caught my first really big bag of bream ($148\frac{1}{2}$ lb. in four hours fishing) many of the local anglers rushed to tell me how lucky I was . . . and that I would never do it again. Well, they were wrong on both scores. I was not just lucky, I had put a vast amount of time and effort into searching out the bream shoals and in making sure that when I found them I would be suitably equipped with bait and groundbait. And I did do it again, many times. In fact, from 1957 until I moved to Kent in 1965, I did not miss a season without taking at least one individual bream bag of over 100 lb.

When I first started to fish the Medley—a water from which I have taken literally tons of bream—few anglers realised its great potentials; now, I suppose, that in angling circles it is one of the best known bream waters in the country.

On any stretch of bream water there are what I call 'holding swims'. These are swims in which, from time to time throughout the season, the bream will congregate and often remain for a period. These are the swims often referred to by anglers as 'bream holes', and they are usually heavily fished. They may not be 'holes' at all, but will usually be located in the areas I mentioned earlier, bends or bays being particularly popular.

These are the obvious swims to look for as a starting point.

Unfortunately however, bream shoals are not static: therefore, the fact of having found one of these 'holding swims' by no means ensures that you will find the bream at home. To add to your troubles, it is not easy to decide whether they are, or not. If you are lucky you may see the bream moving. This can take the form of gentle 'rises', rather like a crafty old trout rising daintily to a fly, or it may take the form of a powerful leap from the water. The latter can be spectacular both in quality and quantity. To see a bream of 4 or 5 lb. come out of the water like a rocket makes you wonder why people call them sluggish: to see a really big shoal priming is a sight that you are not likely to forget. I have been fortunate enough to see many shoals of bream priming and never fail to be impressed. Perhaps the largest shoal I ever saw was at Eynsham. I was fishing just below the point where the Canal stream enters the Thames and had little success during the evening. As the sun dropped and I thought of packing up, I became aware of a vast amount of activity upstream. For at least a hundred yards, the water was practically exploding with bream. There were literally hundreds of them, hurling themselves from the water with complete abandon. Needless to say, I was back there the following evening . . . and enjoyed tremendous sport.

If, having chosen your swim as a likely one for bream, you should then see a fish or two moving, it is usually worth settling down to 'work the swim up'. That involves fairly consistent ground bait until the fish come on, and then, possibly heavy ground bait to keep them there. I always carry huge quantities of groundbait for bream fishing and, even so, have had to leave the fishing to replenish it on many occasions when the fish have been really 'on'.

Although I say I prefer to choose a swim and fish it out, simply because I hate staggering along the bank festooned with tackle and weighed down by groundbait, I only choose to do so when I am sure that I am amongst the fish—and that is when I can either see them moving in the vicinity or I am, in fact, catching them. Otherwise, I keep on the move. I do put in a lot of time locating the shoals, either by walking the banks and looking for them moving, or by fishing all of the likely spots in the area. It is a wearisome business moving swims every half hour or so but it is often the only way of finding the fish.

I usually move about thirty yards at a time, giving each new swim about three 'coconuts' of groundbait placed close together and about half an hour's fishing time. Unfortunately, one cannot give guarantees and you are quite likely to see at the end of a fruitless day of swim searching, masses of bream priming in the swim you started out at! The fact that you are not catching bream is by no means a guarantee that they are not there. Shortly after the big catch I mentioned earlier, I fished the same stretch of the Thames with three companions. Derek started in the swim which had produced the bag with the intention of 'sitting it out', whilst the remainder of us ranged about trying likely spots. At the end of the evening we were all fishless. Derek decided to move, and being somewhat tired, I dropped into his swim. My very first cast across the river produced a bream of 5 lb., of course, it was then a case of 'everybody in'. Between us we had over 100 lb. in something less than an hour. I don't know what the explanation is: it may have been that Derek was casting to the wrong spot (all bream swims seem to have a 'hot spot') or, as I consider more likely, the bream may have been activated by a change in the stream caused by the opening of lock gates on the weir.

One important point to realise when bream spotting is that very often they prime when they are on the move from one feeding area to another. If this is the case, you can be fairly certain that they will not stop until they have reached their destination. You may pick up the odd fish or two, but generally speaking, groundbait thrown at a moving shoal is wasted.

I think the above fact explains the seemingly opposed views one hears expressed about the relationships between feeding and priming. Some anglers say that if they are priming they cannot be caught, others state quite the reverse. My own view is that if you see them and they are moving, few will be caught—if they are priming in a settled swim, that is the time to make a bag.

I have had quite a lot to say about bream, partly because I am particularly keen on bream fishing myself, and partly because in my experience most of the anglers who visit the Thames are keen to come to grips with some of its deservedly famous bream shoals. But, of course, bream are not the only fish to be caught during the summer months. Many anglers concentrate on barbel, chub, or roach, and even more are quite happy to fish for whatever may come along. Barbel, in particular, offer some tricky problems and, on occasions, terrific sport to those who are prepared to specialise in their capture.

Although the Thames has been long renowned for its barbel fishing, the visiting anglers and, indeed, many anglers who fish the river regularly, have little idea of its true potential. True, quite large bags of barbel are still taken from time to time, and in most matches the odd barbel will be caught, but not the quantities one would expect from the head of fish which the river holds.

Just before the beginning of the season huge shoals of barbel may be seen at various spots on the Thames and on the lower reaches of its tributaries and side streams. One small weir pool on 'lasher' near Oxford attracts barbel in droves during the spawning season, many of them good fish of 8 lb. upwards. One acquaintance of mine claims to have seen a barbel of at least 16 lb. and, as he has caught many around the 11-12 lb. mark, he is a pretty reliable judge.

Where these huge shoals disappear to after 16 June is a mystery which remains unsolved. It seems certain that they split up into small groups and it is likely that many of them drop downstream to settle in swims which one would not normally associate with the species. Certainly, weir pools which one normally associates with barbel are not the only places to seek them; in fact, I have caught many from typical bream swims both in summer and in winter. Visiting the Thames Championship this year (1967) I saw two fine barbel hooked (one was subsequently lost) on the stretch below the bridge at Tadpole in the sluggish sort of water one would hardly associate with these hard-fighting fish.

However, if you really intend to set out your stall for barbel, I should recommend the purchase of a Thames Weir Permit as the first step, for although barbel do spread themselves around the river, you may feel reasonably confident that there will be some inhabiting the weirs at any time of the season.

In fact, the weirs offer excellent value in fishing for any species. Perhaps they are at their best in summer when, quite often, they are the only source of running, oxygenated water to be found. There is one small weir pool owned by an Inn on the outskirts of Oxford which holds a head of chub numerous enough and sufficiently large to be of interest to even non-anglers. Whopping old loggerheads of four or five pounds will rise to potato crisps, pork pies, sandwiches, and even cigarette ends, in the most undignified fashion. I suppose that it is something to do with living so near to a pub.

The average weir pool contains a delightful variety of swims. You may wish to fish in the white water beneath the weir sill for barbel, or the formidable Thames trout; eddies in the bankside and beneath trees may be searched for chub, or you may prefer to fish the steady water at the tail of the weir for shy biting dace or roach. Pike and perch too, are fond of these pools, and I would say that most of the better pike I have taken from the Thames have come from weir pools.

I mentioned earlier that I rarely do much serious roach fishing before September, but they are taken all the year round whatever the condition of weather and water. Oddly enough, one of the best spells of roach fishing I ever enjoyed on the Thames was during a particularly hot and prolonged summer. I remember travelling back from a broadcast with Bernard Venables and telling him that in spite of all the moans I had been having about the heatwave, I had enjoyed particularly good sport with the roach. He too had been having the same experience on quite a different water. It just goes to show that if we fished only when we thought conditions were perfect, we should miss a great deal of sport.

However, in general, my own observations suggest that after spawning the roach split up into smallish shoals and, in summer, in conditions of low water and little stream, they tend to spread out considerably. Later in the year, as the weed growth dies off, they congregate more in the fewer suitable feeding places, but it is not until about February, usually when the spawning instinct is strong, that the really large shoals become established.

Upper Thames roach are not particularly large, on the average, and although a two pounder is an ever-present possibility, a regular stream of fish from say 6 oz. to $1\frac{1}{4}$ lb. would be considered a good sample. Incidentally, although it is often said that roach (and bream too) shoal according to size, I have never found any evidence to prove it. When the average size is bigger with, perhaps, a fair sprinkling of $\frac{3}{4}$ lb. or 1 lb. fish, a pounder is quite likely to be followed by an undersize fish.

The early days of frost and cold winds can put the fish completely down when there is little stream, and the shallower water rarely fishes well. I imagine the fish to be lying on the river bed with their noses in the gravel or the mud, sulking like goldfish in a tank on a cold day. A good stream encourages them to move, but they don't seem to roam so far once established in their winter quarters.

The winter is a time when a knowledge of the river bed proves invaluable. The lily pads of the summer may no longer be visible but their roots are still a source of attraction to the roach shoals. Knowing the location of a deep hole in an otherwise shallow stretch, or the whereabouts of a calm patch of water in an otherwise swirling stretch of river, may lead to the bream. A ledge in the river bed, forming a natural deposit for food, may go unnoticed from the river bank.

On the other hand, a little thought and some time spent in exploration before 'lobbing in' can make all the difference between a good bag and a blank day. With a fair stream running, the set of the water can tell you much of what lies beneath, and a careful search with the plumb-bob can help to pick out the probable location of the fish.

With a fairly fast winter stream I doubt whether the actual depth of water is terribly important. The volume of water in any swim is changing so rapidly that the temperature must be fairly uniform. When, however, you are faced with a slack flow and a sharp overnight frost, it is often worth seeking out the deeper spots. I well remember fishing a match one Sunday morning when just such conditions prevailed. I drew a swim on a shallow reach and, although it usually fished well, the cold snap had been sufficient to put the fish well and truly off. My total bag was $\frac{3}{4}$ lb. and that was not too bad, compared with the general run. After the match I dropped downstream into a narrower and much deeper stretch and in a couple of hours took thirty-five nice roach for a total weight of $18\frac{1}{2}$ lb.

It is often said that you have only to spit in the Thames and it comes over the banks, and it is certainly true that one of the winter conditions with which anglers must learn to cope, is floodwater. When I first fished the Thames I used to look upon flooding as an unmitigated nuisance: now I look to flooding as a means of locating the fish.

In those early days I was presented with two seemingly conflicting lines of advice. One school of thought suggested that one should fish the backwaters and eddies; the other claimed that this was a waste of time as the fish remained out in the stream. Which is correct? From experience, I have discovered that there is an element of truth in both arguments, and from my own observations I have worked out a theory which offers a working foundation for choosing where to fish.

On the same rivers a freshet, or run of floodwater, seems to have the effect of bringing the fish madly on the feed, but this is not true of the Thames. I have never known the river to fish well when it was rising quickly. In fact, the effect of the first stage, a swollen and rapidly rising river, is to put the fish off.

The period when the river has reached its maximum height, and when the fish have not had time to become accustomed to the extra rush of water, I call the second stage. The fish are temporarily forced out of the main stream and seek refuge in any pocket of still water, no matter how small; they are not yet prepared to move far from their normal winter haunts. At this time, small eddies along the banks, in sedge beds, or cattle drinks are well worth fishing. In these conditions I have taken good chub and bream from pockets of water which looked too small to hold them.

The third stage may be said to begin when the stream begins to fall and fine off and the fish have had time to become used to the extra volume of water. At this stage they begin to venture out into the stream again—often hungrily. This is the time when legering well out in the fast water or, perhaps, on the edge of the fast water, can produce some magnificent mixed bags.

But what I really look forward to is stage four, and this only occurs after a prolonged spell of flooding when the river has been gushing and swirling along for a week or more. These conditions tend not only to move the fish from their various winter quarters, but to congregate them in more permanent retreats such as loch-cuttings, backwaters, gentle eddies and, in fact, any convenient area of comparatively still water. I know of many such floodwater swims which I would not dream of fishing until there has been a period of prolonged flooding—then they fish magnificently. I have had some wonderful bags of roach, bream and pike from them, and very often tench and eels too, even in January and February. These places are obviously worth looking for and I always keep my eyes open when summer fishing. Providing that he knows his water and is able to read the signs, floodwater is a great help in solving the Thames anglers most difficult problem, that of locating the fish.

Printed in Great Britain by The Press at Coombelands Ltd., Addlestone, Surrey